THE GAMBLER

**Stories of gambling, psychology
and advice for redemption**

Andrea Falcinelli

Notes/Dedication

To my father Vittorio ...

An incredible man who with his mixture of simplicity and crazy genius taught me to live.
Thanks to his trust he taught me to keep myself out of serious trouble and away from people who are negative.
Thanks to his generosity, he taught me that wealth is relative and when you want to make someone happy, especially a child, little things and thoughts are enough.
Thanks to his artistic side he taught me that rationality and numbers are not enough to be satisfied in life.
Thanks to his expressive and vocal opinions he taught me that compassion is both talent and quality, making it one of the most appreciated qualities of the people I meet on my path.
Thanks to his risk appetite (albeit more moderate than mine) he nevertheless taught me that if I had been lukewarm and totally averse to risk, I would never have gone far in life.

Advices and indications that today make me feel alive and happy, because at the age of 38 I have already visited more than 30 countries around the world, because I had to learn how to manage by myself living in Asian countries, because I have lived endless new experiences, new loves, passions.

I feel I have lived and have been living in other lives, all of them within my own life. My father's scent is so strong and imprinted between the nostrils and the mind that I will never be able to forget.

Thanks Pa!

Welcome to the Casino

www.andreafalcinelli.com

universethanks@gmail.com

 @andrea.falcinelli.author

PREFACE

And so, the "Peter Pan" Dr. Farnesi, the bullied boy Giacomo, the beautiful Korean woman Aurem Lee, the easy-going Iolanda, the charming "Wolf of Wall Street" Harvey and myself in first person, we will try to make you identify with our stories of gambling and redemption. We will try to make you understand the dynamics that determine gambling addiction and the exciting and hard path that must be taken if you want to live together with that side, using self-control.

Sometimes when the addiction is chronic and truly destructive, it is not possible to live with it. If this is this case, drastic actions and the help of loved ones or professionals in the sector of addiction will be needed in further support.

Here the reader will be able to understand the most common sensations and feelings that shadow the minds of players and lovers of pathological risk, there is no exemption regarding age, sex, race, cultural or socio-economic differences. It is easy to doze off and let yourself go into the vortex of this fun and devious addiction.
So, if you are not a player but you suspect that a loved one

may be, do not hesitate to deepen the observation of the critical symptoms that I list and dissect in this book.

Personally, I really hope to be able to give my contribution to help someone solve their problems with gambling which unfortunately often affects the harmony and stability of entire families, both because of economic hardship and because of behavioural changes, that generally disfigure the personality of the victims of gambling addiction.

Life is wonderful, a unique journey on our natural paradise called Earth. Anyone who is a slave to an addiction sees the world and everyday life in an increasingly limited way. Life begins to be lived only as a function of this dependence and in the case of the topic addressed here, money becomes pure obsession, when both are compulsively invested to obtain quick gains and are then destroyed without restraint in attempt to recover losses. The loss unfortunately tends to become heavy and unrecoverable, eventually destroying the life of the player at all levels; social, economic and personal. So how can a human being, as the highest expression of talent and intelligence on a universal level, waste his time becoming a slave to an addiction? We just can't afford it whatever kind of addiction it is.

As anticipated in this book I will try to recommend the best ways to attempt a redemption or at least to manage the phenomenon, then to put back freedom and talents at the centre of each of them, which determine the real success of the personal life mission. Trying to stem depression and self-destruction, the "risk lover" will have to learn to control his impulses by listening to the indications suggested by his own conscience day after day and, if that is not enough, opening up to external help.

Today's society doesn't listen, support and easily integrate the most sensitive personalities who are precisely those at the greatest risk of falling victim to addictions.

If you are a gambler your new life mission will start right here, at the end of this book, at the end of the tunnel. Because your true-life mission is already written and you just have to go back to marvel at the simple miracles of every day, to discover your infinite potential and your ultimate talent. It's time to go back to life, as a winner! Enjoy the reading.

THE GAMBLER

FIRST PART

GAMBLING AND GAMBLERS STORIES

- 1 -

RISK ADRENALINE AS A DRUG

Here you will find some stories about my life and how my risk appetite has developed, confirmed by the story of some of my experiences with gambling. I will tell you about a short love story of mine with a Korean girl who suffered from heavy gambling addiction and I will tell you the stories of other players of different ages and social backgrounds, all this in attempt to analyse the vice of gambling that often for me will, or by mere destiny have crossed my path.

In this way we will end up touching on psychology and philosophy as an inevitable step to look within and better manage this propensity to risk that should not be condemned but defeated or managed like any other addiction. This project needs to be metaphorical, comparable to all the other addictions that modify people's lives negatively by altering the perception of reality.
So, you don't have to be a pathological gambler to appreciate its ultimate purpose. We just have to take note that when an addiction dominates us, our nature is

changed, we lose sight of our personal and virtuous attitudes becoming victims of a degenerating passive cycle.

Many vices or perversions if taken in moderation can have beneficial and relaxing effects, for example the game can give a little relaxation away from the repetitive and stressful everyday life, adrenaline and pure joy when you win. Some abuse with shopping, others with too much work, others are simply lazy, and laziness becomes their immobilizing addiction.
And still many people abuse food and alcohol by fuelling diseases such as obesity, diabetes or alcoholism.
Others abuse drugs, those who get lost in social networks, on TV, in endless sessions of video games, and then someone who can even become addicted to compulsive sex.

It is all relative, and the sums invested in one or more of the above examples can be significant. But the problems are not limited to the loss of money only; in my opinion the most serious waste is in terms of time, health, job opportunities, travel and certainly relationships with other people that deteriorate or are destroyed permanently. There is so much to lose in many ways. But in this book, I will talk about how all the negative aspects of an addiction can affect the life of the most sensitive personalities, using gambling and financial risk in general.

So, when we abuse something the cause is inevitably dictated by a problem that occurs upstream, in real life. Once we enter the negative loop of an addiction it will be important to admit it quickly and with extreme humility, otherwise we will find ourselves trapped in the grip of masochism and victimhood, that will grow hand in hand with the defeats and related economic losses.

When we don't solve the real problems that crowd our subconscious, intolerance, disappointment, isolation and boredom will push us to abuse something, quickly becoming dependent on it regardless of the type of addiction itself. Personally, I have been to Casinos in Las Vegas (3 times), Prague (2 times), Amsterdam (2 times) and Macau (1 time but for 26 days straight).
In these paradises of the ephemeral I enjoyed intense and pleasant gaming sessions, sometimes winning, sometimes losing.

I have often played in online casinos directly from the sofa with the PC connected to the TV, for me it was certainly more exciting than a TV series or most of the football matches of my favourite team, despite the latter two being pleasant activities that I often enjoy during the year.
How could I ever judge the horde of gamblers that populate society? A billionaire business gambling that has seen the birth and growth of cities and casinos around the world that does not experience a crisis year after year, on the contrary they are expanding thanks to support technology that gives birth to increasingly exciting and more enticing games.

I have tasted the adrenaline of a thousand victories and the discouragement of total loss, and everything happened in a few hours driven by the "ecstasy" of risk.

Making and unmaking thousands of dollars just for the fault of not being able to stop, listening to the greed of wanting more, and fast, now.

Lack of balance and boundaries punishes you most of the time and I know about it well. Other times I have been cold and calculating by multiplying my initial budget by 3, 4 or 5 times and then withdrawing, inflated, and elated by the great profit, also by my grandiose self-control.

The moods and financial conditions upstream can also affect a player's performance.

However, I am convinced that losing in a bad way can be useful in life. It makes us reflect, change, push us towards new directions that we would never have undertaken in ease and constant well-being.

I have personally blessed certain failures and drastic changes in my past that if they hadn't happened, they wouldn't make me who I am today, they wouldn't make me travel as much as I have so far, and as a result my wisdom would never grow (definitely not a life guru but trust me, but better than how I have been in the past).

The sensitivity of our evolved mind as human beings leads us to reflect on the reason for self-destructive events, and so we understand how of primary importance it is to remain free, never enslaved by the irrepressible impulses that materialism push us to do. Paradoxically, addiction to work can also hurt, when in order to grind out profits, and perform at the top, always and in any case, people are reduced to alienation without being able to fully enjoy life that in the meantime slips away.

We will find ourselves elderly with some homes and a nice bank account, and what more can we do then?
Strength, beauty, clarity, courage, opportunities and friendships, everything will tend to have changed for the worse. We are not steel machines with a programmed brain, we are human beings who without a psycho-physical balance, perish quickly.

Without chasing dreams and small goals that vibrate with our true inner soul, on the frequencies that we feel ours and with the people we feel in tune with us, we will end up draining our talents and gradually our happiness.

In this case, with the words of this book I want to try to tell you that we can't allow gambling or financial risk in general to take too much of our time as well as our money, and not to become a systematic loser.
It is time to manage the compulsive factor that ruins most of the heavy and repeat gamblers and investors, it is time to know how to calculate your limits, it's time to admit that sometimes you perceive the luck around you and the

miracle of an unexpected win happens, but this is not systematic and cannot be driven to exasperation.

Otherwise, the concept of luck itself would not even exist, which is, by definition, casual and uncontrollable.
But the player strives to believe in something that is not real but something that he creates within his new world of illusions, he believes he perceives the luck around him when he was only driven by the need to play, by mere addiction. Is not possible to know when "is the right time" to take risk in the world of gambling, which is nothing but statistics, accounts and where obviously the chances of winning are always higher for the dealer or for the business managers (as we will see shortly). We are also addicted to all those times in which we insist on a project without having properly evaluated its potential.
Let's think of a business for example, supposing we want to launch it without having calculated all the related variables.

Suppose we believe in it only because we feel lucky or because we perceive that the premises where we want to grow it are energetically positive. Then our feelings are wrong and that seaside bar we thought could make us rich turns out to be a failure. Or let's assume idealistic nature lovers who want to open a winery both for passion and to create a business.
But after endless investments and a couple of years with zero profits, we realize that we have planned

everything on the wrong soil that grows bad grapes which consequently leads us to bottle a bad wine.

When we admit our personal failures, such as these two used as an example, we will already be bankrupt, we will have been addicted to the wrong dreams and blind to the evidence of numbers. It causes us to become systematic losers in the most disparate fields of life because the deepest part of ourselves wants to indicate a subtle malaise that we harbour within, to which we place a repeated, stubborn and therefore destructive resistance.

It's simply time to change our lives: ending a relationship that doesn't make us happy and that makes us live at a low energy level, draining our energy, or maybe it's time to change a job that is sapping us of every psycho-physical strength and only gives us back stress and tension, or it is the time to start saving the money we generally squander by investing it in a project or a passion that is exciting to us, or even start a new life on another continent.
Everything can be changed if the time has come to free ourselves from everything that does not make us live at high energy levels, in serenity, in balance, in health and in love. Just as any noble human being would like.

We said that the addictions that can affect a human being are many, but in principle they all work on the same brain receptors and with the same chemicals that dominate our emotions. That is why becoming chronic gamblers by losing large sums is technically the same as becoming a drug addict, or a compulsive shopper, an alcoholic, or very obese, I repeat, technically.

All disorders that involve addiction derive from a conscious or sub-conscious state of saturation of our will, denote dissatisfaction and lead the subject to punish himself, become ugly. We don't have the will to change or the courage to allow the new situation to develop, so instead we close ourselves in that regressive vortex that creates an addiction, self-destruction due to the inability to let ourselves be abandoned to a natural evolution.

Dear friend who has a gambling addiction, I must tell you that you have only one choice! React, change, find your talents and thus follow your beloved life mission!

And the dear game that seems to be your oxygen today? Calmly, at a later time, you can maybe go back to the casino once a year, or bet a few euros on football match, or do some financial trading, but only when you are stronger than your chronic addiction, when you have eradicated the causes and you will be living in your new winning dimension. So maybe you will go back to gambling only a couple of times a year on leisure trips, or on a special evening with a business partner, or risk a few Euro at poker with long-time friends. Or you, financial trader friend, who lost everything, maybe you will go back to investing a small capital in weighted financial operations, for example in innovative crypto currencies, as

commodities of blockchain technology company or in new start-ups that design robots to clean the world from plastic, who knows?
Rewarding the innovations of the pioneering companies behind a great project could become your new investment strategy.

Once you have found your balance you will also find endless opportunities for success, it's a principle that always works.

ONE CAUSE AND MANY BECAUSE

Why is it starting with playing a few Euros that you can get hooked? Why are we convinced each time that we can recover what was lost? Why do some gamblers start to feel a perverse form of pleasure even when they lose? Why will a habitual loser turn into a chronic loser? Why will the pathological gambler start to lie to himself and his loved ones? Why is it so difficult to escape on your own and do you often need outside support to do it?
The answers are coming from a "risk lover" who has wallowed for years in the world of gambling and financial trading, one who has alternated euphoria with disappointment, and then decides to lie down in the sun of that safe beach called "balance", the so-called play responsibly. I interviewed several people during my trips to Las Vegas and Macau, to Prague and Amsterdam.

Neighbours on slot machines or green tables that like me have bounced between the ups and downs of the game, all experiencing at least once the disgust and the burning disappointment of resounding defeats.

Let's dissect and analyse together the "pathology" of gambling so that if you are a heavy player you can go deep inside yourself without shame or fear, looking for the causes that push you to be so compulsive.
And eventually you will understand the magnificence of

the word "awareness", being aware that the pathology has taken over and must be moderated by using the negative experiences of the past to change for the positive, rebound and then rise again.

Happy rebirth to all of you warriors!

PS. I personally still go to the casino or gamble online but stick to set budgets and regular timelines. So, in the event of a loss, I do not create inconvenience, and in case of a win I give myself some small credit.

Then when I meet my childhood friends' I never miss a good poker game in their company, because in the company of real friends you only bet € 10/20 per person which is more than enough to activate that adrenaline and that competition that makes everything more compelling.

To conclude this postscript, I remind you that playing for significant amounts with friends (even if they are longstanding) can ruin friendships themselves!

Money truly remains the lowest form of energy that we can find in this world and is often the primary cause of conflict between human beings. Money is used to quantify and exchange objects or services, but it will never be able to quantify and exchange experiences and feelings between people.

Niccolò Macchiavelli said:

"No great conquest has ever been achieved without taking risks"

In this brief statement Macchiavelli talks about risk, which is the drug that enslaves gamblers, that bastard adrenaline of which one soon becomes an employee. So, let's convert this adrenaline of risk into a more noble risk, that is the one necessary to regain personal freedom!

This would be an achievement! Scared huh? I know, is hard to do it by getting naked and admitting your limitations, how much shame, but it's the only way to redemption, to get the freedom that will really make us winners.

Risk in life can be an ally when it serves us as a push to make the leap, when our good idea in what to invest could lead us to success, when a good investment could give us a financial income.

But the risk must be weighed. In regard of gambling, financial trading, and all forms of high-risk investment, we generally find ourselves playing with unequal weapons. We find ourselves competing in the face of a petty, false, and always at a disadvantaged risk.

The Administrators of these investment projects including the game's big businesses know the same risks of the game and the returns are designed to autonomously make them a profit. The companies that manage casinos, lotteries, banks, large financial empires, etc., all of these know very well that for every 99 losing sheep there will only be 1 winning wolf.

You can no longer be submissive slaves to these powers that are as authoritarian as they are silently legalized, you cannot fight with a noble sharp sword if your opponent keeps you at gunpoint with a sniper rifle. But you can play and risk with cunning and cold blood, but only when you want to have fun for a while, and without expectations, aware of the fact that you will start at a disadvantage.

If we talk about investments, on the other hand, we will be able to believe in a project only when we are in possession of concrete and plausible information.
Or at least when investing in a possible high-risk project that does not create financial problems in the event of partial or total loss of the amount involved.

LET'S LOOK IN THE MIRROR
AND WE WILL NOT BE AFRAID AGAIN

Dear readers after countless experiences in the world of financial trading and gambling I would like to share some analysis with you. Obviously with these I hope to be able to trigger a reaction in you, if you feel the definitive need to get out of the suffocating trap of gambling that perhaps has already reduced your lifestyle. Or if you feel that gambling is becoming a more and more serious problem week after week, loss after loss. If, on the other hand, you are a pure reader (not a player I mean) interested only in examining this topic as if it were a novel or a book of applied psychology, welcome anyway, welcome to the perverse world of gambling.

Here you will understand the control that gambling can exert on people and all the repercussions it can have on the life of the individual. Perhaps reading this book one day you may find yourself helping someone dear to you who has fallen into the trap, you may even recognize the symptoms. You know, is not at all easy for a chronic player to admit that the situation is getting out of hand, evolving into a real pathology.

No person dominated by an addiction will lightly admit to being enslaved by that addiction.

This book would also like to be a good read for anyone who loves hearing real stories that are told to respond to real needs. As we said before "the dealer always wins" and except for the rare cases where luck, mental strength, experience, self-control, knowledge of the subject and "talent" reward the few professional winners, generally we will find ourselves positioned in the large pool of "losers". On average, for every shrewd winning wolf there are 99 losing sheep.

The problem isn't dramatic as long as we can at least be foxes, that is, as long as we can manage our finances wisely and play just for a little personal pleasure and glory.
Here we are in the peaceful case of those players who bet the classic € 2-3 for lotteries per week, or a few coins on sports betting or online poker. Is not bad in this case.

But more and more often this wise and amusing participation in the game turns into a real and profound pathology. The excitement and pleasure of risk can escalate into chronic addiction. As with any addiction comparable to the use of drugs, our brain tends to lose contact with reality, and not being happy will open the doors of our deepest and darkest side. The dark side where fears and all the blocks deriving from the ghosts of the past come together.
It can be a feeling of inadequacy due to our non-aristocratic social background that we have suffered since childhood in the presence of the wealthiest, or the insecurity we feel in

relation to the standards of success demanded by today's society, or perhaps the failures experienced; loss of job, a love, a trauma suffered during childhood, upbringing too prohibitionist, loneliness or even boredom.

We thus feel the need to be or rather "feel" winning in something and the game can give us this temporary illusion. But if we fail to control the aggressive drive triggered by the desire to play again and again, isolation and loneliness may soon ensue and thus, defeat after defeat, shame and disappointment can flourish.

If the losses become huge, despair, depression and paranoia could also ensue, with the consequent fear that loved ones will notice.
Wouldn't it be better to seek success in fields where we could truly excel thanks to our personal talents?
Certainly yes, but if you are a pathological gambler you have already embarked on the perverse path of repeated failure. The list could be extended a lot but even if the temptation is strong, I have tried not to go too far into psychology and psychiatry, it is better to stay with the various points that we will address to make myself better understood.

It will be your task to gradually analyse yourself in depth and become a bit of a psychologist of yourself by finding the reasons that led you to isolate yourself in the world of financial risk. So, in the following chapters I will not be able to help but go back to touching on philosophy and psychoanalysis, I apologize in advance if I will appear repetitive, prolix, emphatic or confusing at times but it is not easy to dissect these topics. So welcome aboard!

Let's tackle all the most important knots to solve together by immediately taking note of your limitations but also of your potential that can lead you to success once you have come out of the slavery of exasperated risk appetite.

We are human beings, and we make mistakes, through the mistakes and crisis of life we can rebound towards personal fulfilment in the fields where we know how to excel.

To get started, here's what you need to do in the self-analysis work:

> - **Admit** your weaknesses and look inside yourself as the first necessary steps to know your limits and then overcome them.
> The humility in admitting that you are going through a moment of inner revolution that cannot be dignified with immobility and free fall, but only with self-analysis and openness to change.
>
> - **Recognize** that the shame and judgments of others are real nonsense because you were born free and your madness is also part of your genius. Are you a stupid gambler or an immoderate financial trader? Are you a systematic destroyer of money?
> Patience, from now on this is just the past and you

can resurrect into your new strong and balanced personality.

- **You have** to recognize that until you push beyond your limits and these errors are victims of past patterns, potentially you could also remain trapped for life. Many chronic players who have ruined their lives declare that it is impossible to get out of it and that the desire to play will remain with them forever. Damn, we're not talking about heroin that changes the brain almost chemically! I hope not!

- **Transform** yourself from masochists and self-harm into brilliant personalities with talent and passion. It is time to go back to daring to achieve a new kind of success. Thus new energetic, positive and successful people, will cross your new path because they are attracted by your new vitality.

- **Send** gambling addiction to another place and get out of this prison once and for all or at least control its impact thanks to a new awareness. Risk only for fun and occasionally, with pre-established budgets that will not adversely affect your financial balance.

Laziness, idleness and vice, are very pleasant, but when they last too long or become everyday lifestyles, they will begin to wear us out, sooner or later our warrior spirit will push us to implement a profound revolution to find the right stimuli and get back on track to the right path of life. To be reborn in a new phase of a radiant and active life where we again become the real arbiters and administrators of our present, and thus of our future, abandoning the rottenness and errors of the past.

We are living beings with infinite mental power and we have all the qualities necessary to get up and return to smile, produce, invent, succeed, love ourselves and then love!

I conclude this introductory chapter by adding a very important thing that I want you to subscribe to right now. I can tell you about my experience and the feelings, then tell you the stories of some people I met in my experiences in casinos, and again I will give you some advice of course, but I cannot replace tools that are sometimes necessary to overcome difficult challenges such as the pathology of gambling.

Often a discussion is needed with someone close and dear who can listen advise and support, in the work of redemption. Or maybe you need to join therapeutic paths in appropriate structures with professionals who are experienced in the treatment of these pathologies: talking about it with your family, partner or close friends is certainly the first step.

But sometimes even this may not be enough, and you will have to be assisted by associations, recovery groups supported by psychologists and/or psychiatrists, bodies that provide well-trained personnel for the fight against chronic diseases.

- 2 -

THE "NEVERLAND"
IN THE "LAND OF TOYS"

That attraction to the wonderful world of gambling was very strong, whether you were playing in a casino with its surreal, luxurious and sparkling charm, or whether it was on the TV screen with the computer connected, playing comfortably on the sofa. Whatever the context, drinks and cigarettes could not be missing. In the first case both consumed comfortably inside the casino, in the second case the drinks consumed comfortably on the sofa but the cigarettes on the balcony of the house, perhaps lit before starting an exciting bonus session won at the slots, or after a hefty win at online roulette. From gambler to gambler then I ask you, but how can you give up all this pleasure and fun? In that lonely peace or maybe just exchanging a few words with the player opposite if we were at the casino or in a slot room.

"But what pleasure and fun!?"

Psychiatrists, psychologists and good people, who have never played and never will play, will thunder!

So, what makes gambling an addiction & addictive?

Certainly, his ability to produce dopamine first (pleasure during the victory) and then adrenaline (fear during the defeat). But for a less "chemical" and more "psychological" view, I will try to answer in the name of the most avid players who will probably share my analysis, at least a good part of them. All those who hate gambling obviously cannot accept any nuance, cannot see any positive side of it from any point of view. Repudiating any form of risk (especially when the odds of winning are objectively unfavourable) they criticise the "stupid" players who jeopardise personal financial and mental stability.

These people who are so moralistic, perfectionists, who live in their society full of rules, perfect laws and goals aimed only at material growth, see gambling as a thing for miserable people, of low social class and with an objective stupidity, pure masochists.

We certainly cannot criticize them, long life to them and many successes I would like to say, but in turn they do not have the right to judge those more sensitive or less fortunate personalities who find themselves overcoming these challenges, even if they are not very great as in the case of gambling. In fact, think of how high the percentage of gamblers is from poor families or with poor education or in low paid, low-profile jobs is.

In the crowd, however, there are doctors, luminaries and managers seduced by the thrill of risk and high-paying investments, but statistically they are quantitatively lower for obvious proportional reasons.

So how can chronic gamblers take so much pleasure from this risky and harmful practice?

And then is really true that the gambler is always alone and a human waste?

So unintelligent and so masochistic?

Is he really so weak and loser that he starts loving defeat to the point of self-destruction?

Maybe there is something much more complex and subtle that pushes the human being there? We have said that a strong contribution to the dependence on the risk is given by the dopamine released from the brain during the winning, a hormonal boost with a power that cannot be underestimated.

When a particular subject is living a period of life where personal satisfactions are few or nil, or if the subject is used to the successes and victories of the past, he will look for new paths to satisfaction.

Risk is certainly one of them. To this process will be added the perverse action of adrenaline, that whenever the player is faced with the loss of his budget, it will push him to try his luck, over and over, again, to fight that terrible despair. He will again go in search of a dose of dopamine given away by any victories.

This will open a vicious circle that is really hard to break.

In this chapter, dear gamblers, I will be your advocate, the devil's advocate, precisely because I have been, and sometimes still am, a gambler like you. After all, only those who know each other intimately can understand each other and then help each other. I want to try to describe in words the deepest feelings and the motivations that push the "risk lovers" to self-punish themselves to the bitter end, even when they may have managed to win for a certain period. The problem is that the chronic player is already aware of the fact that sooner or later even that kind of luck and therefore regained money, will be disintegrated by subsequent losses and defeats.

Because those who are pathologically addicted no longer know how to be satisfied.

GAMBLERS OFTEN GENIUSES AND HYPERSENSITIVE

Many of the best philosophers, painters, writers, actors, lovers, in short, the best artists were and still are particularly sensitive and often have perverse minds.

Is very easy and equally unobjectionable, to note that all the most brilliant, creative and again I repeat, sensitive souls have complex personalities, and problems in accepting the social contexts in which they are forced to live.

Especially in today's society that seeks to impress its own rules and dogmas on humanity as a whole.

Without these actions it would be impossible to accelerate with globalisation and consumerism. So, for these brilliant and hypersensitive personalities the problems often arise from the thousand questions that sooner or later arise, existential, personal inner questions or even about the fate of humanity. Or reflections on why they are forced to do repetitive work every day that kills their real talents (talents they may not have yet managed to identify in the oppression of the routine of standard life).

Or personalities who find it difficult to continue to endure social or sentimental relationships that they no longer feel alive in, thus ending up denying even the very context in which they are forced to live, that house, that city, those relatives, that job, with that partner who they no longer love. Personalities who can no longer bear that kind of life. Whether or not the strict respectable bigots who point to gamblers as basically failed elements like it, I tend to evaluate risk-loving and masochistic people (given their work of self-destruction) in a diametrically opposite way. I'm not saying for sure that they are better, but I argue that they have infinite potential and irrefutable personal reasons that it is not up to us to judge.

People who are irreproachable and almost perfect according to social standards, perhaps the best physicists, mathematicians, engineers and chemists, such as psychologists and psychiatrists, athletes with perfect physique, all of them cannot judge gamblers only by their self-negative result; destructive and bringing no social progress.

Because behind the players you can still hide talents that the modern age and the challenges of the new generations badly need, but they are not put in a position to express themselves. Our problem or rather one of the problems of today's society is that of not being able to favour and create the conditions and situations that can lead to the enhancement of the single individual.

Without the enhancement and harmonization of the potential within every human being here on planet Earth, how can we hope for a total evolution of 100% of the population?

Obviously, it is unfeasible.

The dependencies and self-harm sometimes become the only way for hypersensitive people, the way to die and be reborn again, it seems a paradox, but the human subconscious goes in search of a personal crisis for their release from conditions in life that no longer vibrate with the real attitudes of the individual himself.

Gambling addiction is not so difficult to identify in a person with whom you live in close contact, you can see it in the shy eyes, in the shy attitudes, in the isolation and in that new and damaging way of managing one's finances.

But if we see or hear "alarm bells" we can become heroes in our own little way, sometimes a little listening and a few smiles are enough to redeem a lost soul.

We understand that we cannot save the world, so if the victim puts up too much resistance it is best to pass the ball to professionals who can try to heal them.

Let us remember that sometimes we may end up with the person we are trying to save, especially if they are dominated by addictions at an advanced stage.

Many people after destroying all their money and sometimes being surmounted by debt, become suicidal as it is hard to keep themselves in countless nightmares caused by serial defeats and misery. There comes the desperation that today is often ignored due to the widespread indifference among human beings, it would take more altruism to save many lives by creating a new attitude in humanity itself. There is no longer the gentle culture of listening, of advice, of sharing problems, of communication as a natural social embrace where those who put themselves at the service of the other from an emotional point of view feel satisfied and satisfied with what has been done for his neighbour.

It is an attitude yet so beautiful and inherent in the intelligent man. More common is the busy man running somewhere focusing their energies on their own satisfaction and personal fulfilment, the ego is huge.
In my opinion, helping someone else to open up from the inner point of view is a deeply intimate thing, not simple, but one that gives unparalleled emotions. Finding people willing to listen is like finding pure diamonds, very rare.

Today it is preferable to point out a gambler as a social issue that creates problems and enters this destructive vortex only through his own fault and cowardice, therefore he does not deserve any respect. The same treatment that is reserved for people marginalized by another nature and therefore addiction. As with drugs, with sex addiction (an addiction that may sound unusual to you, but which really exists and which I talk about extensively in my books on love, sex and awareness), addiction to alcohol and all the others. more or less known, the gambler does nothing but shut himself up in his illusory world. In that virtual world where one goes to take refuge to keep away the causes of his unhappiness and to stay away from the distortions of today's society.

THE BET OF DESPAIR

So even the gambler unconsciously curses the harsh laws of today's modern society and prefers to think like this:
"I gamble everything I have with the knowledge that the chances of losing are much higher than in those to win. I'm there to risk! I just want to isolate myself in a virtual world where I can detach myself from reality, stare at a screen savouring the thrill of getting a bonus on a slot machine that will give me emotions through potential winnings, savour the pleasure of seeing good cards in a poker hand and challenge the other idealists who are marginalised like me, bet a string of chips on that green cloth with the spinning wheel full of numbers following the ball, a ball that will decide my misery or my luck.
In this fictional world, I, as a player, hide, I realize myself and I despair."

And again ...

"So much of that damned money comes from the work that I hate, no longer gives me any stimuli, which repeats itself every day as if I were a robot. I am so full of debt because I have failed as an entrepreneur and now, I can also go bankrupt completely. So even if I wanted to change my future, I can't do it, because I have a family and children that I have to honour.
It is too late to be happy and independent again"...

But I just wish I had a new chance, to be free again as a child. Let me fly free like Peter Pan, here on my Neverland. But I know I can't do it, I have no escape routes from the slew of bills, expenses, and relationships that I have to respect. It is a mortal sin to separate, and what will become of my children who will cry and hate me.

But for me the love towards my partner is over but by now I have signed that document called marriage and I have to honour it, so I have to reduce myself to loving someone by compulsion, by past choices. Oh!

What pretentions in this society today, living in this sweltering city. So! Let me play, drink and smoke until the last of my days!

There are those who have the strength to get out of all this, to escape and start a new life by taking risks and responsibilities, those who are shrewd and indifferent, but there are those who let themselves die inside for one, or more than one of the reasons above.

When addiction and desperation merge the player just wants to be left alone, perhaps sometimes with his drink in hand and with an abundance of cigarettes that emphasize the taste of risk and the state of perdition.

Here we have used gambling and betting as arguments, but we could equally talk about a player on the stock exchange or a financial trader who gambles everything on high-risk investments (I always want to remember this). In any case, let him enjoy when he wins and especially when he loses. Let him rejoice when he wins and he knows he can play a little longer, while remaining in that world of muffled and surreal isolation. Also let him die inside when he loses everything and knows that he will have to return to that real and competitive society, and will have to get more money, which obviously he will return to invest in the land of gambling toys. Let him do it until he has lost almost everything, when he has bet the last desperate euro that remains in his wallet.

So, it will be, until he has the courage to say that he can no longer go on and will have to confide it to someone, or maybe until someone finds out and manages to unhinge the door of that ephemeral world where the player is trapped. Because as we all know Pinocchio arrives in the Land of Toys (we all know that fairy tale very well), and the gambler could not be a more suitable representation since he often too becomes a serial liar with anyone who tries to investigate, just to stay safe in his perverse self-destructive world.

There in the suspended dimension of the Land of Toys, of the famous "Neverland", like Peter Pan, another eternal child. Now I would like to tell you some stories of people who have had serious problems with gambling but who have found the strength to get out of it in different ways, for equally different causes of addiction.

Stories that have been told to me by acquaintances or by those I have met during my travels to casinos or on information sheets relating to the same topic.

Obviously, the names are fictional, and their stories are fictional, and adequate to provide you with a better readable content. The four stories I am about to tell you begin with the birth of negative and frustrating feelings on the part of those who have experienced such disappointment, shame, loss, despair and depression. Then all parties will find the way of revival in a rapid and total transformation, almost waking up from a nightmare, thanks to the trust in someone, with openness, understanding and acceptance of the problem; liberation from the burdens endured and then total renewal.

Others have only postponed the problem for a few months or years, remaining covertly dependent.

Others live with the attraction to risk but have learned to manage it by making it more harmless. But the fact remains that each of you has the infinite potential necessary to solve any addiction problem that comes your way in your life. Never reduce yourself to becoming a victim of shame. Because we are all perfect just as we are, but sometimes our sub-conscious forces us to close the cycles of the past even through sacrifices and dramatic choices. All this to force us to change a life path that was wrong or that was right before, but now it can no longer be so. Because many of us evolve, some first, some later, and obviously also some never. But for those who can make it, blessed be the support, understanding of those who believe in them.

- 3 -

DOCTOR FARNESI
AND HIS SLOT MACHINE LOVER

A very respected Head physician at the Milan hospital with a "model family", 2 grown-up daughters respectively of thirty-one and thirty-four years and an adorable wife focused on giving her all only for the good of the family. Doctor Farnesi could not have asked for anything better from life, let's say that he had done very well at his task of being a good father and providing for his family's needs.

The two daughters had already moved away from home choosing to study in two different faculties respectively in Bologna and Rome, the wife between home and work had entered the typical routine of "housewife" and as she got older, she let herself go a little from an aesthetic point of view.

The relationship between Dr. Farnesi and his wife had therefore become devoid of passion and involvement both from a sentimental and sexual point of view.

However, he was not the type for lovers or prostitutes, so his workload become much heavier, especially because of his cold relationship with his wife.

By now their co-existence only acted as mere glue for the family union. But the physical and chemical attraction had run out. It had been a while since the doctor had gotten into the habit of stopping at a shiny new slot machine room located near the Milan station. He could shelter his mind from work thoughts but above all from the emotional ones, without having to face the sad and inquisitive looks from his wife who waited for him at home every night.

Sometimes he smoked his 10 or 12 cigarettes accompanied by red wine or cold beer, complementary items served by the waitress of the betting room, it was all so perfect in that peaceful and hidden slot room. Farnesi therefore used his particularly hard work commitments in the hospital to cover his playful raids in that new "oasis of peace".

He went there almost every day, in the early or late evening depending upon commitments.

This situation had further stiffened the relationship between the two spouses as the impatient wife had started asking several questions to that distracted husband.

The practice of sex between the two had finally disappeared and the acid behaviour of the wife had made her husband angry and unfriendly. At the same time, she had begun to talk about her problems to her sister, who tried to reassure her with phrases of circumstance, but even the suspicion that a mistress was involved had germinated in his wife.

When their daughters came home from their respective study locations for holidays or free time, they had clearly noticed that serious cooling among their dear parents. Things that the children feel, and in that case the absence of irony and lightness in the father's communicative style was enough, like the less joy and desire to chat on the part of the mother.

A real state of crisis was now obvious between the parents. Those conversations so short and cold between Mum and Dad, during the few remaining family meals, pushed their daughters to ask what was happening to the poor and grieving mother. She tried to hide it all but in a not very credible way.

So, the worried daughters asked the father directly who reacted with hysterical smiles and forced reassurances of circumstance, in fact with his historically positive and joyful personality, he tried to divert the faults of that conjugal cooling on the now advanced age and on the great responsibilities, that his long-lived career implied.

Justifications that were not enough to stop the alarm because there were too many nights when the father came home late, often even skipping dinner.

The daughters had not lived permanently in that house for years, but the few days spent in that context were enough to decree the state of crisis between their parents. The doctor's wife decided to investigate by starting to check her husband's jackets and briefcase.

More and more she found strange rectangular tickets, all white with printed barcodes, euro amounts, and that surprising heading "Lucky treasure slot room".

At first the woman did not give much weight to the clues found, thinking that the betting room was just the typical place where you can bet on football teams or horse racing, a very common vice among men.

She imagined a matter of a few minutes a week and a few euros in spending; certainly not a place where her husband could spend hours and hours.

The frequency in the findings and those strange euro amounts printed on the damned ticket increased suspicions, often the figures imprinted on the tickets were pennies (of course they were the hundredths of a Euro residues after the sessions in which the doctor lost), but sometimes a few hundred euros, albeit rarely. In the meantime, Dr. Farnesi lived in that artificial world of his; gloomy, full of distressing and repetitive thoughts, the depression was advancing but by now he could no longer get out of his relationship with slot machines.

It all started with such pleasant and satisfying sensations, that relaxing haven where you can try your luck with the adrenaline that skyrocketed when a slot machine paid well, and then the thrill of trying to reinvest your winnings in new slots. But after 3 months of play, the evenings of strong disappointment had become too many, where in three or four hours the doctor had burned more than € 500.

At first it seemed to him that he had become an expert connoisseur of the winning cycles of the machines and that he had acquired pure clairvoyance skills as he often managed to choose the best moments to try his luck, with excellent consecutive wins. In the early days as a gambler, he was also very good at self-control and being able to stop when he wanted. But now he had accumulated 3 months where the losses far exceeded the winnings, moreover even when he won it had become really difficult to stop, the tendency was to risk more and more in order to cover the regressed losses.

Thus Dr. Farnesi truly began to feel a failure, now he was apathetic, alienated, disheartened and defeated internally. The "shit", that every heavy player sooner or later finds himself ingesting, had also been served to him on the plate of addiction. The doctor felt more and more a loser, both as a citizen towards society and as a father towards his family. Perhaps it would have been better if he had taken a crush on another woman so maybe he could tell the truth to his wife and, albeit dramatically, try to start a new life.

Actually, because the cause of his isolation was the will to isolate himself from his wife, who Farnesi just could not bear from the family and sexual point of view. But the dear doctor had no relationship with other women so his sentimental unhappiness had led him to take refuge in the game without anyone knowing, in that slot room he could find freedom, protection and that beautiful adrenaline rush from risk that was now missing in his daily life.

In the early days of gambling, as we said, the doctor did not give weight to the financial expenses that gambling involved, in fact, despite being in the deficit of a few hundred euros, he was well covered by his excellent salary and by his huge savings account.

The bets were minimal in the first few weeks, a pastime where, by betting fifty cents at a time, you could spend more than three or four hours gambling with € 100 or € 200. And what a thrill when from the initial one or two hundred euros he managed to take away three, four or five times as much. But as mentioned above the wind had changed and self-control was wavering.

It was the fourth month of play and in a couple of weeks he had already burned € 3,000, but the miracle was coming, finally luck came knocking on the door of Dr. Farnesi giving him a great windfall! One lucky evening in late autumn the doctor hit a pretty hefty jackpot in one of his favourite slots that earned him € 2,850 in one go.

He received the compliments of all his companions in misfortune, that is the habitual players of the slot room where the Doctor was now best known.

Many retirees, middle-aged entrepreneurs fleeing business stress, single women, sometimes a few passing kids with snack money to invest, or non-EU citizens in search of their much-needed fortune, all in turn in the world of that dominated hope from pure statistical cycles.

Will the slot pay or not pay? But who cares about others? It was Farnesi's evening.

The doctor offered a drink to a couple of players with whom he had bonded over time and enjoyed that incredible rush of adrenaline, cold sweat, hands trembling with emotion while the hypnotized eyes of the "traveling companions" stared at the magnificent win drawn on the screen of his slot machine.

What wonderful sensations!

Like running to the cashier and changing that ticket with € 2,850 written on it.

His wallet was full and after playing another fifty euros on the same slot machine, to verify that he had not missed any other winnings (typical practice of the most sensitive gamblers), Dr. Farnesi went home, fully satisfied.

Calculating a lump sum total of four months of playful activity on the slot machines, the doctor was in deficit of about € 6,000. But a positive evening was already a good sign of luck to try to keep morale up, after all he had lost € 3,000 in the previous three weeks alone. Sometimes it seems that it is life that manages us, even if it is hoped that it is always the opposite, yet how many events happen without asking our permission, and happen with such a perfect and therefore frightening synchronism. And that night, when he came home the doctor found his wife waiting up for him, ready to go to war until she found out what was behind all those absences.

She was sitting at the table with a chamomile tea in the kitchen and he couldn't help but pass in front of her in an attempt to reach the bedroom, so the woman's questions started straight away without any welcome greeting.

She asked her husband if he had any problems with gambling, if it was appropriate that at his age he behaved like a little boy, destroying his life and his savings on gambling, if he still had a shred of love for her and for his daughters, for the whole family, understood as a union and institution.

He tried to deny it at first but when his wife waved a penny note she had stolen from his jacket pocket in his face, he froze and fell silent for a few seconds.

So, she felt strong and rightly began to denounce to her husband all the shortcomings she and her daughters perceived, and the folly of the fact that a highly respected Doctor like him had chosen to throw himself into gambling. And he raged by throwing a lighter on the table as a symbol of misery for the fact that he had even started smoking.

He, feeling attacked, accused her that there was no longer any feeling between them and that she had participated in the decline of their marriage with her taking everything for granted, in addition to all the things that as a woman she should have to take care of to keep herself attractive to her partners eyes.

And again, he said that there was no woman, there was no person as the cause of their separation, only that the game was enough to make him feel better, in solitude and in peace. A vitriolic conversation that sanctioned the definitive break between them.

She raised her head and looked him straight in the eye for the first time, because she hadn't been able to do so from the beginning of the conversation until that very moment. He was still standing with his jacket on stopped talking and returned with an equally exasperated look. And so, his wife asked one clear, dry question in a trembling voice:

"Now you have to choose! Power! you have to choose between me and the game! So, who do you prefer? Me or the game?".

The doctor remained impassive and cynically replied: "I choose the game! No doubt! ". Taken by a mixture of adrenaline and perverse euphoria (emotions very similar to those he felt after a big win at the slots), Dr. Farnesi returned to the front door, went out and drove away to reach an hotel in the city, where he spent his first night as a single gambler. No clothes to change, no briefcase, only the night of marital destruction.

He felt a mixture of severe shame and adolescent happiness, on the one hand he had just destroyed his marriage and family cohesion, on the other hand he had full and total freedom without having to act and hide what he really was, at least in that phase of life.

The humiliation of the desperate wife was so great she did not know whether it was better to discover her husband as a gambler, or to discover him in bed with a mistress.

She called her sister explaining what had happened between crying fits and then next, she tried to sleep but that was ruined with pain and by the abundant tears shed. From that moment on she did not see her husband for a long time.

The doctor had dropped the bomb, he was alone, ready for a new life where the newfound freedom pushed him to be positive and innovative looking to the future.

Not knowing unfortunately, that the biggest challenge of his life had actually just begun; that of the addiction to gambling. The night of the argument with his wife was also that of the big win of almost € 3,000 in cash; and that money was squandered by the Doctor in just 2 days.

Taken by the euphoria of his newfound freedom, the Doctor went wild like a crazy horse on gambling, with sessions of 4-5 hours in a row and bets of every single play that varied between € 1.50 and € 2.50.

He was convinced that by betting hard he would soon get huge winnings, since sooner or later the machines where he was investing those large sums would have to pay.

But unfortunately, the Doctor persisted in his gambling

operations even on two totally negative evenings that ushered in the most dramatic two months of his life.

The separation from his wife and the newfound freedom was not enough to make him truly a free and happy man. But the financial drama that it was going to cost the Doctor was the price to pay to regain his freedom is the same after such a great personal crisis. It was too late, he hadn't confided in friends, obviously he hadn't discussed it with his wife, but not even with his brother or his beloved daughters. Many of these people would understand, they would help him.

The Doctor in the madness of that new very aggressive gambling method (with bets as mentioned even higher than € 2 per single slot spin), drained his bank account in a couple of months, this time his hands didn't shake with the adrenaline released thanks to the victory, but feeling the desperation of having burned more than € 60,000 in a few weeks.

Ruined by compulsive gambling, he relied on a psychiatrist colleague from the same hospital for which he worked, who, as a friend as well as a professional, helped him get his life back in hand. From a broken man of the game to a new man who still could excel in the work he was doing with love, and a man who would also find a new love for life.

Doctor Farnesi was eventually helped by Martina, a woman with a really fit physique who was known in the gym, that environment had helped him in the work of redemption from the disease of compulsive gambling.

Those who are heavy gamblers know very well the stress, fear, misery, apathy and depression that comes with long and difficult attempts at detoxification. I'm not here to cynically terrify readers who know full well how hard it is to win the battle with an addiction, but it wouldn't hurt to send a warning to those who are starting to feel a little too assiduously drawn to the risk, the one described in this book about gambling is like risk in any other form.

I conclude the story of Doctor Farnesi by reiterating that the people who can listen to you and help you in the challenge against gambling addiction are already around you.

They are the ones who enhance your best qualities, who smile at you with an easily perceptible sincerity and who love you for who you are despite the fact you may make mistakes.

They are your children, your best friends, your parents or your co-workers. They can be identifiable in anyone you feel connected in a particular way: those who know how to listen, those who know how to play things down, even when others would see everything in black, all the people who have the ability to put themselves in your shoes and then take you by the hand and accompany you out of the tunnel with full confidence.

- 4 -

GIACOMO THE "BULLIED" BOY

Poor modern society with all these psychological problems, communication problems, respect for others and what hurts the most is that it is mainly at the expense of adolescents and young people. In youth, sensitivity is extreme, and one should only live carefree in harmony with others, sharing positive and never traumatic experiences. One day the competition and having to look at all costs pose young people with new forms of stress, depression and apathy, many kids do not find the motivation and incentives to show their talent. In this situation of precarious psychological balance plus other hazardous factors, such as lack of rules and even a basic education.

Thus, the prevarication by the more aggressive and rude guys on the weaker and more respectful ones is now very "fashionable". The responsibility for this social situation is also attributable to those parents who no longer have the ability to "say no", the teaching of humility.
It would be necessary for children to learn to absorb sacrifices and defeats as facts that happen during the course

of life. Even my generation, can remember bullying and abuse impressed by those teenagers from the "strong character" (and without the quality of an educated family behind them), to the mildest and most submissive personalities. There have always been situations of mockery and humiliation on the part of some towards others, threats, extortion, heavy insults or even severe physical violence.

I remember this very well, is not science fiction but issues happening in many school environments.
However, we are not here to deal with the evolution of bullying over the last few decades, a subject as important as it is impossible to dissect in one breath here, it would take a whole book just to address the scourge of bullying and its evolution with the advent of social networks.

Now I 'll tell you the story of Giacomo, a fifteen-year-old boy attending the classical institute in Rome, passionate about art and literature, always with a beautiful smile on his face. His parents, coming from middle-class families, tireless workers, the mother a merchant and the father bank employee.
Giacomo was an only child, respectful of the rules and without any vice or self-centeredness to show off, he was simply a typical good boy. To go to school, he travelled the same road every day on his moped, preparing to face the morning with the usual stop at the large bar near the study centre. A bar used as a meeting point for many students of

various social backgrounds and adhering to different study fields.

The typical bar owner prepared rich breakfasts for all palates, with a large selection of pizza, focaccia, omelette, brioches, sandwiches and stuffed sandwiches, products that students just "can't live without". From a back door the bar continued to extend into two large lounges.

The first used for playing cards, billiards and live football, the other, a home to more than twenty slot machines and a cash desk whose business was money exchange and for players to collect winnings. The same cash desk was also equipped as a bar for the administration of drinks exclusively to the players hosted there. Access to the slot machine room was theoretically forbidden to minors but the insiders turned a blind eye in most cases.

Profit first of all!

Giacomo was an intelligent boy and was wary of any stranger who wanted to take advantage of his goodness and integrity of soul, unfortunately, however, his good academic performance and his aesthetic humility had placed him under the attack of three classmates with petty lives. They were skivers and consequently had poor academic performances.

It all started during the first year of high school and that harassment would then last until a good part of the second year of attendance.

Almost daily the three bullies unleashed their envy and their cynicism on the good Giacomo who was holding up that heavy and humiliating situation with great fortitude.

Dickhead, ass-face, shit-ass, lousy toilet and nerd bastard, were just some of the names they called him.

Please excuse me for the impropriety. Every morning before, during and after the lessons Giacomo had to hear such profanities, screamed or whispered, sometimes he had to read them on his books or on sheets of paper carefully stuck on his back. Another practice adored by bullies was to create small balls of paper soaked in saliva and then throw them at the submissive companions.

For the launch they used BIC writing pens, in fact once the contents inside the pen were removed, they became tubes with amazing ballistic qualities.

The drama increased during the five-a-side football matches held during physical education lessons, when the poor boy was bullied with kicks, pushes and balls unloaded on his body with unprecedented violence.
The bullies did not have the objective of scoring goals, but only to forcefully unload the ball on the body of the bullied kids. Part of the class tried timidly to defend themselves and to defend Giacomo who was targeted almost daily, but the arrogance and terror ended up being unleashed even on those who tried to oppose the supremacy of the bullies.

Giacomo's parents together with those of other weaker students had already reported the situation during the previous school year, however the principal and the professors could not do much more than admonish the 3 insolent children and their families.

Paradoxically, the situation had worsened at the intervention of parents, professors and the principal, and had unleashed further hatred, threats and harassment against the oppressed. The practice of the typical mafia-style silence. It was precisely from the middle of the first year of high school that Giacomo endured that heavy situation, the summer break between the first and second year had served to make him forget part of the wrongs and oppression suffered, but the beginning of a new school year was upon us. The second year had started with the same nightmare scenario and were once again sitting in the same classroom as Giacomo. It was hard not to react to the constant psycho-physical violence and his dazzling smile had now turned into a shy cover mask.

Giacomo was dying inside day after day, emptied by so much violence and too much injustice that raged on him for no reason. He wondered every day why life was giving him such harsh treatment, where he went wrong and how he could get out of it.

Towards the middle of the second year his scholastic performance had significantly worsened, and the boy had started to call in with various absences, sometimes due to illness with the approval of his parents and sometimes of his own will falsifying the justifications, therefore without any real permission.

I really think that you dear readers can guess where Giacomo stopped to spend the mornings in solitude, obviously at the bar described above, more precisely I confirm that the young man had become an avid visitor of the slot room at the back. The fear and nausea that seized him every morning at the thought of having to go to school, led him to take refuge in that slot machine room where he could spend some time in peace, at least until lunchtime when he could go home. In a few weeks Giacomo had burned about € 2,800, which were the savings accumulated over the years, including odd jobs, gifts from relatives or his parents themselves.

It was all the cash that he had set aside with sacrifice and perseverance to fulfil his dream of a first transatlantic trip to the United States of America.

From a dream to a nightmare where his treasure was burned morning after morning due to that damned gambling addiction that had become chronic in record time, an addiction that was also the only escape from the depression that was eating him inside.

Giacomo's parents started to become suspicious and only to understand his serious psychological fragility when the professors revealed his scandalous academic performance after the first term. It was already February and, unfortunately, they had not noticed anything before.

The malaise of their dear son was hidden behind his hermeticism, behind his surrender, behind the fear of denouncing again, a complaint that could have cost him further fury by the bullies. Giacomo had tried to react in the first two months of the second year of attendance, in fact, even skipping a few lessons he went to lessons with decent consistency, enduring the usual oppression.

Unfortunately, noticing that Giacomo's absences increased week by week due to their pressures, the bullies had continued in their destructive practices forcing him to absent himself further.

And so, weeks of learning and hundreds of Euros were going up in smoke, also speaking of smoking we must add the fact that Giacomo had started smoking to kill time and stress during his long morning gaming sessions, with additional expenditure both in terms health and economic terms. Paradoxically, the smoking became a saving factor as this smell on the son's clothing began to make the mother suspicious, a suspicion that added to the shocking and alarming revelations from the professors who notified her of the collapse of the son's academic performance.

And so, for Giacomo's parents it was easy to understand that the model son was going through a dramatic moment in his life that could have led to serious and irreparable consequences. The poor performance and the frequent absences, all realities unknown to them up until that moment (in addition to the fact that their son had started smoking), were sufficient evidence to push them to urgently open a wide-ranging dialogue. It was one evening in late February when Giacomo's parents began to ask him direct questions about his academic performance, the absences he was having and why he had started smoking. On that occasion they could not be accommodating, they could not ask questions of mere circumstance, at that moment the two good parents wanted to make their son confide in them without the possibility of escape, even if those direct questions could have caused him further pain and humiliation.

Giacomo taken in check by the three dry questions posed by his mother under the equally inquisitive gaze of his father, lowered his head staring at the centre of the table, then raised his shining eyes again towards his parents and began to cry.
This began his monologue of despair. A river in flood that overwhelmed the parents, a cascade of painful stories about the last year spent under the psycho-physical humiliations by the three classmate bullies, his escapes at the bar, the mornings playing slot machines, the vice of the smoke that began in that gloomy and lonely context.

His mother followed him in a cry, not so much liberating as Giacomo's was, but dictated by pain and sorrow for the suffering of her son. The father listened to every detail of the story believing him on every single word, after all he was still "his Giacomo" the model and integrity student, before his personality was marred by those thugs.

He got up from his chair and went to hug him while the mother still in tears held both hands of her son who was dripping from his eyes and sobbing.

But now Giacomo finally felt free and light, protected by the love of the parents who had unlocked him.

Now it was time for those adult people such as the parents, the professors and the headmaster to clarify every detail on those terrible past and present issues, repeated over time, it was time to resolve the situation once and for all, without fear.

The anger of his father could be felt all around in that kitchen as he explained in a powerful tone all the actions, he would take tomorrow. Here's how the situation evolved in the following days: the three bullies were called to acknowledge the abuses and repeated violence on poor Giacomo, who found himself a victim two times, once to the bullies and once to gambling. Now it was time to rebuild for everyone. The bullies were shamed in front of their parents and had to pay with the loss of the year and the suspension until the following year. The chats on the various social networks that Giacomo kept were a terrible test of everything he had to endure, proof that therefore he ended up severely punishing those three boys who acted strictly in groups with choral bullying actions.

Thus, further stories of bullying emerged that the three thugs practiced in parallel on other children who were victims of the system. Giacomo was strong, he had only had to endure a heavy test that perhaps life had submitted to him in an attempt to make him grow, probably with that incident he had forged himself, it had been a pledge to pay to further develop his sensitivity, now he was ready to become the man of art, communication and positivity that the world needed. And Giacomo took his life back in hand.

Behind a gambler there is often a winner in life who has only decided to give up for a moment, a sensitive and special soul who has had to undergo and know the ghosts potentially hidden in his deepest "I" (IO), to then analyse the true meaning of life. In the contempt of money, in the pleasure of risk and then in the repeated loss, many players understand that love and nature are the true miracles of life, all connected with universal love.

You can see faith and religions as you want dear reader friends, but every God you can worship must reside in love, and it is enough to spread the word of this God who wants us to be happy, fulfilled and healthy.

Trust today if you are a lost gambler, talk about it today, your new "me" is ready to surprise you.

You have nothing more to lose, right?

Did you burn a lot or all of your money?

It's done, it's over!

Are you feeling any increasing discomfort due to losses from betting, trading or any form of gambling more generally? Well, you still have time to turn it around.

- 5 -

AREUM LEE
THE KOREAN ENTREPRENEUR

Between Korea Macau and Danang (Vietnamese city on the sea, hosting some casinos), these were the movements that Areum Lee used to make in the last 3 years.

Some new business opportunity that took her to Macau had gradually changed her life in Korea as a successful manager in the fields of catering and cosmetics.

Her new opportunity was to provide cash for Asian players who were massively assaulting the photocopy city of Las Vegas, let's talk about Macau.

More precisely, the limits on cash transported on international flights, some stringent financial laws and even the limits on credit cards, they needed intermediaries to exchange large amounts in local currency.

Areum carried out this transaction work to the limits of legality, because it was this that the most avid players needed to be able to bet large amounts in the casinos of the city, that is, of transactions that could be defined as "legal". Miss Lee had started working for some of the most important casinos in Macau where she met players interested in obtaining cash, after payment of a commission established by the casino managers.

She received a percentage fee as well as some important benefits if she also wagered a certain amount of money in the same circuits as the casinos themselves.

For example, she could stay overnight on full board for entire weeks in the luxurious 5-star affiliated hotels (the same concept is used in Las Vegas).

Here are the rules that these under-the-table deals between Lee and the casino directors were not obvious and which were by no means negligible since as always, they were to the advantage of the house.

Specifically, to guarantee the free stay and the related benefits I mentioned above, Aurem Lee had to make a minimum of bets every week in order to accrue the bonus points necessary to cover these benefits.

Everything was accrued on a common ATM-style magnetic card where the game points were credited.

So, in addition to the work, she did as an intermediary for the cash exchange between casinos and customers, our Korean friend was encouraged to gamble on her own and at her own risk with her own money. Honestly, it is not clear if she was forced to join this sort of double job, of which the second part is totally at her own risk, or if it was, she who chose to set up this life in Macau. Evidently, she could have decided to live in some modestly priced apartment and only carry out the activity that the Casino required in the beginning, without risking her own money in gambling.

But she liked to gamble so she was probably trying to combine business with pleasure by taking advantage of the free stay at those high-class hotels, and so by gambling she hoped to be able to obtain further profits.

The daredevil Miss Lee would relax during the day by shopping or taking care of her body, waiting for a call from loyal or new customers (a call that could come at any moment).

The evening and the night were reserved for a few drinks in the most prestigious cocktail bars and of course for gambling. She was passionate about Baccarat and incredibly managed to win large sums thanks to her experience, her instinct, the well-analysed statistics and certainly also thanks to the luck that often sat on her side. This happened in the early days but obviously it couldn't have lasted forever. Areum Lee preferred to play in the casino of the City of Dreams complex, at the Venetian or at the Galaxy of which she had the loyalty cards that allowed her to accumulate their respective reward points.

Therefore, jumping from one casino to another guaranteed whole months of free stay thanks to the practice of her second profession, with a good contribution also from her third profession, the gambling.

After a few weeks in Macau, she would generally return to

Korea to spend time with her mother, with friends, and check out the other businesses she mostly ran remotely.

She tried to avoid returning home in the winter months as she had a difficult relationship with the harsh climate that often caused her flu. A viable alternative to both Macau and Korea was the city of Danang in Vietnam, a sunny seaside town where the cost of living was particularly low despite the quality of life itself being excellent, complete with sea and semi-tropical-style beaches.

Danang was a nice place to take a break and reflect, also because after a long period of success the wind of luck could abruptly cease. At least being there saved on living costs with the added advantage of the low betting limit of the casinos. A lower wagering limit meant less stress and pressure when gambling, especially when compared to the high expectations pressing on her performance in Macau. After a couple of years of this happy and sumptuous life, albeit with ups and downs, between casino gambling and related business, alone or in the company of male friends or partners, Areum was about to run into a violent storm.

As with most heavy and chronic players, the most painful setbacks and the most disastrous economic losses often come suddenly. There is the period in which the gambler is on his honeymoon, skilled controller of his bets, meticulous manager of his financial assets and often very lucky serial winner.

Then something jams, this happens when the first winnings of a certain significance allow the player himself to let down his guard and he begins to believe he cannot lose.

The confident and overconfident player will feel entitled to raise the stakes for further gratification and exponential gains. A process that changes simultaneously both at the cerebral chemical level (endorphins and chemistry linked to pleasure and success) and at the economic level (sums invested gradually much larger). And here we have reached in a single month, or in a single week, or in a single day or even in a single night, total defeat.

By risking more and more, aiming higher and higher, the losses grow and thus self-control deteriorates to the point of losing touch with reality. At that point the brain sends more and more intense revenge impulses, the need to recover all the losses in one fell swoop to wash away the fear and anguish, push the player to double, quadruple or tenfold the stakes up to extreme cases where the desperate player will come to stake everything he has left.

This is the last act, he will remain in his underwear, desperate and humiliated. The luckiest players will leave safe at least with their savings in some investments not immediately available, others will cry desperately for having burned all the cash they had.

Returning to our Korean adventurer, she was about to face a gradation of this desperation just described, she still didn't realize that one cursed night was ready to steal months and months of profits, plus all that burnt time bouncing from one casino to another pursuing the mere profit. A night ready to steal her security, her esteem and her beloved reputation. As much as having a good reputation in Macau casino dress was worth, it certainly was worth to her and it was important to keep it.

It was the first days of March 2018 and Aurem Lee felt an unexpected melancholy, accompanied by restlessness, yet in the previous weeks she had been particularly happy because she had met a boy. He was smiling and positive, spiritual but at the same time very open-minded, he had travelled to many countries, especially in Asia.
They met thanks to the dating app "Tinder" and so they spent a few romantic days together. She sensed that this meeting was not by chance, he was a very different type from those she had previously met, he had the ability to read her inside. Lee had already told him what she did in life and her new boyfriend had already understood that that life of business, casino, money and a lot of friction around her, kept her far from simple happiness.

But he also understood that she was too closed, proud and a nationalist person (a common feature in Koreans) to let herself be saved, to try together a path out of that vice of gambling that had turned into challenge and addiction. I wrote "exit route together" because that European guy knew the world of risk just as well as he was a part time financial trader and a hobby gambler.

But he could fully understand the pitfalls of gambling addiction, he also knew the pitfalls that await every risk-loving person following lucky (but temporary) victories. He had seen the excitement in the eyes and words of his new Korean love, because she insisted that she could make a living by gambling, because with calm and steadfastness she was convinced that she could dominate the game of gambling at baccarat.

But he had also seen the coldness, the apathy and the fear that enveloped Areum's soul when he came from a night of defeats and losses on the green cloth assisted by the state of intoxication of the ingested spirits.

They had fallen in love sharing their weaknesses, but it didn't mean that love could be long lasting.

It could be the typical mutual need to find answers, to look inside each other and accuse each other, to rise to the Olympus of love and then fall down quickly once they come to terms with personal inner ghosts.

Because there was perhaps too much pride among them. For Miss Lee it was the time to reckon with herself, while her boyfriend could only make her understand how the sadness, the isolation and therefore her rigidity in denying those gambling addiction problems, would neutralize any feelings between them, as well as ruining her life more generally. From a sentimental point of view, he was a rather shrewd subject, it could take him a moment to fall in love, showing all his typical Mediterranean passion, but just as he fell in love quickly, he quickly ended relationships. Because he was a man of the world, a traveller who had had relationships with over 200 women along the way, one who lived by instinct. Each time his feeling was that his soul mate, the real one, was waiting for him at the next stage of his personal and spiritual evolution, and so the years passed between one relationship and the next, none ever seemed the perfect and definitive one. But he was still 36 years old. Miss Lee was 43 years old, although she physically looked half of them thanks to her white skin of Asian silk, and the miracles of Korean aesthetics.

The first times they spent together had been wonderful, even full of plans for the future with pure idealism.
They had enjoyed remnants of the warm and fun Thai life, as he lived in Bangkok where he had hosted her for a few days. But soon she showed signs of uneasiness and an obvious withdrawal crisis for her life between money business and casino gambling, so soon she left for Hong Kong first and then Macau. According to her, the passage to Hong Kong was necessary to move some capital into an account she had opened there.
He stayed in Bangkok, hoping to see her again soon because he had the feeling that he had fallen in love with her. But it was just a feeling.
The drama erupts a few nights later, unexpectedly, a real story that I am here to tell you but not before revealing

another twist, dear readers, and this is the right time to do it.

That Italian boy who lived in Bangkok and was infatuated with his "Korean doll" is me, Andrea Falcinelli, who is writing to you here to raise awareness on the pitfalls of gambling and how to overcome it.

We are all potential geniuses, all winners and all potentially adept at moderating ourselves and getting out of negative situations.

All like me, like Areum, like Giacomo, like Iolanda, like Doctor Farnesi, like Harvey (the characters you have read so far and you will read later), all gamblers, misunderstood geniuses and sensitive souls in evolution. Yes, I wanted to insert my relationship with this ex-Korean girl (who obviously has another name and surname) because the coincidence or connection (call it what you like) is incredible. Just me with my experiences in the field of risk on this person's path.

I hope you don't hate me if you ever read this book, through which I talked about a part of your life, about the two of us, but it is an act I felt I was doing to try to help other people in need. So, I just wondered over and over how life had brought us together with such a synchronism, for such a perfect project, both united by the vice of the game.

It was almost as if she had been chosen to make it clear to me and to make it clear to her the same thing could lead to gambling addiction and share this story (like all other interviews and stories included here) to help chronic players. We were partaking of that drama, of that night in mid-March when she began to write me a flood of messages on Whatsapp, where she told me cryingly that she and I could no longer be together. That our love made her fragile, that thinking of me she could not be strong and win in the game of baccarat, that soon she would block me on all lines of communication we had because it was right, because it had to end like this, and I had to excuse her. Yes crazy.

She was raving, bombing me with little messages connected to each other but I did understand what had happened in Macau, a disaster that she was trying to hide, out of shame and disappointment, towards a rapidly moving farewell. I wrote her some reassuring messages in an attempt, to calm her down and at the same time to understand what was happening, I promised her that together we could fix everything.
I had no answer back until the next morning.

That night I couldn't sleep comfortably because it was one of the rare times I really fell in love and had let down my defences, forget the money, that had never been a problem for me. I had lived as a rich man, as a poor man, I had won a lot, I had lost everything, I had changed countless jobs in my life and therefore my karma from this point of view was excellent, the opportunities always came up.
But the main point was that I didn't want to lose once again what I really thought was my wonderful Asian soulmate,

after all we even shared the vice of gambling!

Damn, she had seriously blocked me on Whatsapp, my head was spinning from confusion and disappointment, lost in my solitude after that night spent reading the messages written by that strong and fragile Korean girl. Fortunately, in the late morning Lee wrote me on the Telegram chat, an application we had installed to follow some groups that shared information on crypto currency trading.

So Areum Lee told me:

"Dear Andrea, I'm on the ferry to Hong Kong to reach the bank where I keep my last savings to try to recover from a dramatic situation that happened to me last night. Sorry for the harsh and disrespectful words I wrote to you last night, but I was out of control, scared and desperate. I burned 1.5 million Hong Kong dollars on the green Baccarat table in an attempt to recoup the large losses I had suffered earlier in the evening.

I could not control myself, I thought about us and the fact that with a large sum we could start a comfortable and happy life, I don't want to blame our love, but this has happened, it has already passed.

I now owe at least 1.5 million Hong Kong dollars to the casino because yesterday the manager approved a credit in my favour after the first losses that had drained me. In a few minutes I risked all that loan granted to me by the

casino and now I have no escape.
Forgive me and goodbye."

It may seem cynical of me but the first thing I did was to open the currency converter on my smartphone and check how much that "astronomical sounding" figure was in Euros. Maybe some dear reader there among you is doing the same, come on admit it;). Fuck!
It was 169,000 Euros (with obvious variations if while you are reading this book the exchange has increased or decreased in relation to your local currency).
I absolutely did not know how rich or crazy the dear Korean doll was, the fact is that for me it was a huge amount and I certainly could not do anything to help her. However, love had really stunned me because I replied that I did not care about the lost money, and that she could get back on her feet immediately, it was over now but together we could rebuild a future, I did not judge her. At 4 pm on that same day we would then talk to each other via Skype video call.
We did it on time, and she was so beautiful, with that porcelain white face with perfect Asian features, shiny black hair and lips a little too puffy perhaps, but of a natural bright red that in that context was the end of the world.

My Areum Lee, my dream of that time. Despite the drama just experienced the plan was for me to stay for a while along with her in Macau, working on the PC. For this I had a good autonomy, often traveling for pleasure around the neighbouring Asian countries.

From mid-March until early April I would be with her in Macau, residing at the Nuwa hotel at the City of Dream complex. The goal was to reorganize her return to the road by enjoying our time together in parallel, trying to play down what has just happened to her. However, I cannot hide from you that my instincts foreshadowed something negative coming. As you well know these are things that cannot be explained, especially in love, the force of attraction makes you continue to believe in a date even if you perceive that you will crash into an iceberg.
After what had happened to her and then she had confided in me in full hysterics, obviously something had changed between us, more than anything else in me, the illusion of having found a stable, strong and independent woman had crumbled and I could no longer to see a long term or eternal story. So, what did I do? I return to the cynical speech I made a few lines back.

That is, I had no intention of destroying myself by chasing a love spoiled by addiction problems.

I also like to be romantic and believe in chocolate phrases like "meet your partner's ghosts and help her defeat them", or maybe "learn to play with the demons that dominate her heart and turn them into angels", and then "thank you to love you become one and there are no obstacles" and many other fantastic principles. But when it comes to addictions, I am now certain that the initial shot must come from the deep self of the person concerned, the person who has that particular problem on which it depends must want it.

I've heard countless stories where the Red Cross girl was trying to get her boyfriend out of drug addiction, or the guy who was trying to get his girlfriend out of addiction to compulsive shopping, or maybe the story of alcoholics to save. In short, I think that giving primary care, giving clear advice on possible paths to take, and then accompanying a person afflicted by some addiction is wonderful.
But indulging her, making her feel like a victim and following her without opening her eyes is a wrong thing. Sometimes the addiction can be defeated by the person himself in solitude, step by step, but in the case of external assistance the path of commiseration and victimisation never pays off, there is a risk of skipping the precious assumption of responsibility.

The person intoxicated by some addiction tends to lie to others as if same, only focuses on useful solutions obtaining other "substance" that serves to satisfy his addiction. So, it will circumvent and exploit the person who commits it with cunning, we repeat, the goal is only to indulge the addiction. The person a victim of addiction and therefore of himself needs a detached and cynical help that can observe the situation clearly, with professionalism, without prejudices and I also feel like saying with a pinch of strategy. Love seen as redeeming and addictions don't get along very well. For this reason, I already felt that the situation between me and my Korean doll was fading, from an idealised dream we were entering a grey reality on the horizon, full of personal obstacles to face.

She would never have wanted to share them with me admitting her excesses and frailties, that pride quite common in Asian personalities. However, I had by now decided to leave Bangkok and join her, for weeks I dreamed that trip with her from Hong Kong to Macau would materialise. Continue to visit a part of the Asian world that I had not yet had the honour of visiting, this time with a woman I really liked.

That fateful day arrived and so we boarded together on the flight of the Blue Panorama company, business class with priority line and excellent harmony and energy around, after all, when you travel all problems disappear and you just try to enjoy and share beautiful experiences. Hong Kong was magical with its streets illuminated by coloured signs, like Asian writings, the area dedicated to nightlife with fascinating and stylish clubs, a mix of perfectly integrated races.

We always walked hand in hand, my doll and I, and we laughed together while continuing to plan for the future despite everything that had happened.

Despite that feeling under the skin of uncertainty we just wanted to relax and have fun, so much had already happened in such a short time, maybe we both just had to wash away a bit of restlessness.

We were two selfless, sweet and very open-minded people who were both struggling with personal perfectionism, we wanted idealistic love, and we knew that maybe we would break that union as well.

This severity put us in front of many limits, but we wanted at least to live those beautiful moments that would in any case, never return.

The emotions were deep and wonderful. And so, the two nights in Hong Kong were as magical as they were fast, the ferry to Macau had materialised in front of us and it was time to board. We often looked at each other as we sat in relaxation, crossing that strip of sea that separates the two toy towns. Soon we are in Macau, a real Las Vegas of Asia with very similar gambling energies, but totally different people and place energies.

In Las Vegas you perceive Americanism and its inimitable style, originality, in Macau you see Chinese economic growth and the well-being of the surrounding countries, a copy of the Las Vegas system with Asians infected by the frenzy of love for money. As always, I intended to use that time in Macau as a disconnection from real life, don't think about anything for a while and enjoy the idleness, adrenaline and vices connected to that unique context. So relax, play, have drinks, random spins in casinos, search for inspiration for some lucky shots, rest, a bit of the gym, a massage and again starting over, games and drinks, a live show or a cinema, a dinner and more drinks and gambling. How beautiful!

Yes, for a few days is okay but after four or five days that lifestyle also begins to get tight. I stayed there in Macau with my " Korean doll " for 26 days, in that five-star hotel connected to her Casino and then all the other Casinos at very short distances. Long live 26 days in Macau!

Do you realise? Well in the next paragraph I will tell you in summary of how it went.

The first week I could call it our honeymoon.

Everything that was most beautiful happened and without any kind of disagreement, no shocking exchange of views or other problems between us or outside of us.

The 5 stars Nuwa hotel was wonderful, our room was very spacious; but 'perhaps it would be better to call it an apartment as it easily exceeded 100 square meters.

We could order top quality food at any time of the day and prepare cocktails ourselves thanks to a wide selection of spirits and soft drinks in our room. I loved making her my cocktails mainly based on vodka and tonic water which she enjoyed and drank in abundance.

Our favourite to share was the Moscow Mule, that I mixed in my way using: vodka, ice, a slice of lemon, a slice of cucumber, a piece of yellow ginger, some ginger beer soda, and a bit of tonic water.

Refreshing and perfect to lift the turns of our complex and slightly perverse minds a little. So, from the imperial chamber we took the elevator together and, walking a bit through the shopping center, we reached the game room of the main Casino of City of Dreams.

We didn't play together often, in fact she generally spent most of the time on Baccarat while I loved sitting at the Poker Stars tables. Then sometimes we would meet around the slot area to burn off our respective accumulations of adrenaline and tell each other how the evening was going. Sometimes we both won, sometimes we both lost, sometimes one lost and the other won and vice versa, in any case there was respect and joy between us.
I perceived a unique energy as if we were recharging each other, and as if that place, we had carved out far from the world, and from common life, was our real natural habitat.

The third night was the best as I won € 1500 starting from a € 250 budget, right at Texas poker. She slipped a slew of "Players" and "Bankers" to the Baccarat table and smacked me with her absolute supremacy in making money, over € 5,000. Well after all I was a miserable compared to her. My average spending for a year in Bangkok was around € 15,000, including travel to neighbouring countries and all my monthly expenses.
She risked € 15,000 in a single night without any problems, not to mention, as you well remember, her earlier terrible and astronomical loss of around € 170,000.

However, although I was a small provincial player and she was an expert Hollywood film woman, I knew very well the sensations, the absurd superstitions, the strategies, the difficulties in respecting the pre-established budgets as self-protection, and the enormous risk of losing control.

You can play a lot or a little but when you become a gambler, the chemistry acts on the brain in a more or less equal way for everyone, the nuances change.

Of course, there are rare exceptions of personalities adept at winning often and losing rarely, personalities who destroy their entire budget in record time, thrifty players who bet very little just to pass the time.

And so, we could go on indefinitely with the nuances, dear friends, but when you are victims of a real pathological addiction you can react in many ways: controlling it, becoming its slave, entering and then exiting it, re-entering it after a temporary redemption, and many other possibilities to be blurred in the ways and times.

Returning to my adventure in Macau, I resume the subject where I left off, however the rest will be much more dramatic.

I had pointed out how the first two days in Hong Kong and then the first three days in Macau had been fabulous, lived as a joyful couple madly in love.

Then the rest of the first week together continued with some diversions, such as going to lunch in a quaint Portuguese restaurant by the sea or taking long night walks under the moon and the lights of Macau, starting from our hotel and reaching the heart of the old city.

It was like jumping from a very young city built solely for casinos to a small Hispanic European-style village. In fact, the influence of Portuguese colonialism had left its romantic footprints on the doors and signs of houses and businesses and restaurants set here and there in the alleys of that pretty village.

Walking hand in hand for a long time it was pleasant to open up further to each other, talking about our lives, our families, our need to live an exciting life without being under the influence of institutional and religious leaders and rules. We were really in agreement on everything, but perhaps all that agreement could become the very reason for a future separation. Too much independence, too much self-awareness, little habit of compromising, and also a lot of pride. Our willingness to take risks which usually should be a blessing in love, could have burned all the fuel of our love in no time. Those ten days together, excluding the first week spent in Bangkok, were the only ones we could remember in our love diary.

From the second week on, all the negativities of gambling addiction harboured within Areum began to manifest themselves: short temper, mood swings, authoritarianism, impatience, victimhood, frailty followed by tears and even slander against me.

All this was the proof of the profound malaise that my "Korean dream" could no longer manage.

This time she would not be able to hide behind excuses or mystifications, this time I was there with her and her half-truths could not win over my opinions and my lucid analysis, because I was a connoisseur of gambling and its psychological traps.

Twice she accused me of being dangerous for her because I knew how to read her inside, because ex-boyfriends were crushed by her character and her decisions, no one dared to contradict her, and no one had ever managed to unlock those inner secrets of hers.

Days of struggle and resignation of a story that I perceived would end as soon as I returned to Thailand, at least I was once again experiencing a life experience that I love to define "from film", one of those adventures that basically show my inner self.

Moreover, the relative disappointment for what was happening was counterbalanced by the very strong awareness that I had matured within me in the years of new life in Asia. I had learned to be thankful for everything that life offered me, and I had learned to laugh at everything that life submitted to me, the most beautiful exercise that I liked to do then, as today, is to smile looking at the sky and then converse inwardly with God.

For me personally, a God outside of religions, science and earthly rules, a friend who looks at me from the infinite

Universe and laughs at my misfortunes like a spiteful child, but then rewards me with priceless gifts and experiences that I value if I continue to live in goodness, in sharing, in compassion, in unconditional love. And then everything is obvious to me and I can remain happy even when I lose a love that seemed pre-destined to me. And let alone when I lose money or material things, it is no longer a problem, because I know that today they go and tomorrow they come back. In those days of tension, in front of that fragile and hypersensitive Korean woman, I understood that I had been called to her to share her pains and try to move something inside her.

To get her out of that diabolical labyrinth of gambling addiction.

Even if I hadn't succeeded, I would have remained in her memories as a unique person, someone she had known and with whom she had shared a piece of life. Those last three days together were tense, and we swallowed some of those lies that a gambling overdose makes in humans.

After all, she had also gambled the money she had taken from the account in Hong Kong and I had screwed up my budget of one thousand Euros, plus the beautiful win of €1,450 that I had wisely earned playing Texas poker.

There she felt even more bankrupt than before since the frightening amount lost in the beginning (before I arrived in Macau), was added the losses counted in those days with me around. I, who by now kept very little sentimentalism, counted my lost coins thinking about the fact that I could have invested them in a much more profitable way.

Maybe in crypto currencies or by taking a nice month trip to an island of Thailand, enjoying, not a paranoid woman, but a calm beauty without any problems whatsoever.

They were just thoughts, as for now what had been had been and between mutual raising of voices and insults between the lines, we took leave with an icy goodbye at the Macau ferry station.

However, I was happy because an interesting meeting was waiting for me in a beautiful hotel in Hong Kong with a cocktail party in its rooftop bar. In fact, I attended a conference on the EOS Blockchain company for which I had edited the Instagram profile in the previous months. After all, life always goes on and if we learn to play and joke with our inner challenges and frailities we will discover that life itself is a game not to be taken too seriously.

Because what we think, want and absorb becomes what we will do, receive and become. And what happened to the dear Korean doll, you ask? She wrote me some messages on Whatsapp saying that she needed months to "fix her mind", this was the translation of her words in English.

She invited me to join her in Danang in June to try again, because I remained important to her and because she had met me at a wrong time in her life.

Because in Danang minimum bets on the gaming tables were much lower, and so she could gamble there with less

pressure. Start again to do what I thought?
I answered that for myself of course.

Unfortunately, she was still addicted to gambling and out of pride she did not want to give up but wanted to move the battle to a less hard battlefield. I replied that it was a busy period and that in the month of July, as every year, I was preparing to return to Italy for a wonderful month as I missed my family and old friends. I wanted to work a little longer in Bangkok and save for the trip home.
Of course, it was a half the truth as I had no intention of walking with her on a new thin glass floor with my hands full of steel chips.
It would have been easy enough to lose a few chips from our hands to shatter that crystal veil under our feet and fall back into the void of our misunderstandings. And so, after my refusal, everything gradually faded.

I didn't look for her anymore, she wrote to me again in October but with resigned messages of circumstance talking to me about a new life outside of gambling and an upcoming long trip to the United States. I could only wish her the best and take my leave after having exposed the latest news of my life.

- 6 -

IOLANDA LONELINESS
AND HER SLOT FRIEND

Shapely and short, always smiling, loved by the neighbours as much as by her two cats, I present Iolanda, the one who harboured a certain melancholy within her that matured after retirement. A very sweet Italian teacher esteemed by almost every student who had been lucky enough to have her as a teacher.

Maybe she was too good, but she still managed to win the respect of her children by involving them warmly and supporting them even during the interviews, where too many gaps embarrassed the most problematic or less deserving students. After all, teaching in a classical high school she could at least avoid the fearful boys of the technical and professional high schools, historically much harder to manage at every level.

Famous in the school circuit thanks to her arrival at the headquarters in her white FIAT 500 (post 70s vintage model), her strict punctuality and that menthol scent emanating from the candies she always kept in her handbag. Unfortunately, she could not count on the love of family members who over time had hermetically closed themselves in their hectic daily life, her two dearest grandchildren had grown up snubbing her abundantly. With cats being her passion and her most faithful friends, she took care of them meticulously, stroking them on the sofa while reading books, correcting students' classwork, or relaxing listening to her favourite classical music.

Iolanda was a spinster now resigned to her long-term loneliness, first because of the disappointments of love that had psychologically scarred her at a young age, then for the misfortune of not having met a kind of companion of life at a more mature age.

The simple physical appearance with a few extra pounds had certainly not helped cupid in the search for a soul mate, so her love spilled over to the two cats and the students. With the arrival of the pension, that channel of love and usefulness that connected her with the boys was also exhausted, it was not easy to get out of it without paying an additional duty from an emotional point of view.

But basically, her refined intelligence allowed her to have fun with little and to love the simple things in life, furthermore her literary sensitivity allowed her to remedy the carnal vices with intellectual ones, and theatre, art exhibitions, a few evenings at the cinema with friends With these long-time friends, Iolanda shared the thrill of playing cards from time to time, real full immersion in bridge where a few coins were wagered to make the competition more exciting.

However, with the passage of time, many people become lazy and give up, giving up even the hobbies they love most. And that was what happened to the tired old friends of the cards. So, on the one hand, her grandchildren, now grown-ups, deserved her a greeting only for Christmas and Easter in the easy mission of receiving gifts of money from her, and on the other hand the friends of cinema and bridge walked away with the excuse of difficulties in moving because of the ailments and related risks.

She was left with her home hobbies, reading on the sofa with cats now as overweight as she was and some solo outings. She liked to drive her "Cinquecento" car through the streets of Rimini stopping perhaps for a cappuccino, for shopping in the historic centre in her trusted shops, or even at the usual supermarket close to home.
Sometimes she walked along the seafront without a specific purpose, first in one direction and then in the other, or she ventured into the hills until she reached the Republic of San Marino and then returned home by evening.
During one of her pleasure rides one fine day the dear teacher stopped for a session with her favourite hairdresser who was located in the largest shopping centre in the city.

Once the hairdresser had finished the work on her thick reddish hair, she walked slowly towards the large revolving doors that preceded the exit towards the parking lots, when something attracted her. On the left she paid attention to a large, gleaming sign promoting the mall's slot machine room.

That intense blue with countless symbols recalling luck, silk-screened along the entire wall that stretched for at least twenty meters. The large black doors did not allow you to immediately look inside that very mysterious room, but they certainly encouraged you to peek inside, so Iolanda could only slow down for a moment.

Her first instinctive reactions were thwarted, going from an enveloping curiosity to immediate shame.

Her moral integrity and risk aversion came from the indications of the left-brain cap, while the perverse, risk-prone impulses were pushed by the bored right brain cap in search of adrenaline. Something pushed her to cherish the idea of a visit to the slot machines, it was a cloud of chemical impulses between temptation and pleasure, these were supported by the avalanche of flashbacks on the times lived with friends playing bridge.

That rapid antagonistic exchange between nerve endings was undermined by much simpler and more automatic motor-type brain instructions. In fact, if the first pro perdition emotions were followed by a sharp stop of her steps, when the good rationality intervened her feet resumed walking with rhythm towards safety.

So, having crossed the exit door of the shopping centre, she rushed towards the car, placed the shopping bags on the passenger seat and set off on the way home.

A perverse worm connected to that glittering sign of the slot machines room materialized in her mind, but it faded once she was physically back in the house. Another evening of red wine, sofa, books, classical music and cats was reconfirmed as her boring but saving way of entertainment.

The summer of 2018 was now drawing to a close and Iolanda also saw the great opportunity to spend her retirement days at the sea fade away. Also, for that year it was time to say goodbye to the punctual ice creams at 4pm, the crossword puzzles under the umbrella, the regenerating bath at the beginning of the sunset and the pleasant chat with the neighbours under the umbrella.

Boredom returned to dominate the scene.

At the beginning of October Iolanda went again to the largest shopping centre in the city to take care of her body, in the beauty salon where she was a client well known and loved by all the staff. The girls who took care of her had become a bit like stepdaughters, between stories of life and confidences, the easy going retired teacher, always had that right advice or that word of comfort that made her a bearer of wisdom and positivity.

Obviously, the girls also loved her for the timely tips she gave at the end of the session, whether it was a pedicure, a shampoo with hair colour, or a waxing. After her session at the beauty centre, Iolanda stopped for a coffee in one of the main bars installed in the large atrium opposite the parking lot of the shopping centre. Dear readers, I can confirm that it was precisely that hall where a few weeks ago Iolanda stopped for a few moments to stare at the entrance to the slot machines room.

This time the observation of that mysterious place was prolonged, there was all the time necessary to receive her coffee at the table, sweeten it, blow on it a few times and sip it. Adrenaline caressed her cerebral cortex, her heart accelerated briefly and soon the idea of taking an exploratory trip into the world of gambling was imperative, an idea already decided.

With a slow pace, then more and more accelerated, the dear lady went to the entrance of the slot room.

A moment of uncertainty before opening the door that perfectly hid that dark realm, then a reactive click that made her find herself inside in an instant.

After all, the shame of standing in front of the slot room was more powerful than her indecision, moreover, to support them, the adrenaline, the curiosity and the desire to chase away the boredom that had already settled over the years continued to push. A slew of over 50 slot machines lined up in 6 different sectors populated that room which was very dark but with a guaranteed view thanks to the sparkling lights that came from the screens and tables of each "money-eating machine".

The place was all in all pleasant because the players were focused on their individual sessions, so there was no invasiveness, neither visual nor verbal. For the first time in that place of perdition, Iolanda found herself relatively at ease. She just had to choose a game theme that she liked in a machine willing to pay some winnings, she hoped, apparently all a matter of chance and statistics would make every common mortal think, but for the player the perceptions and the instincts are of prime importance. Too bad that the world of slot machines hardly welcomes you for a single session letting you escape with the loot, indeed, as we well know, a possible win, even a small one, tends to push the player to try again.

And in case of loss? You don't want to give up on the first try? These conscious and unconscious circuits are the seeds of gambling addiction, which is relatively easy to get into but difficult to get out of. The way was marked when the new victim sat down in that comfortable chair in front of the chosen slot. Iolanda slipped her first € 50 banknote to play a slot inspired by the gods of ancient Egypt, with the possibility of accessing fun bonuses when 3 to 5 books of ancient Egypt materialize in order random on the game reels.

The bonuses, that are paid randomly, are the rewards that make the sessions even more exciting and therefore addictive. And so, she began to push the button with cadenced frequency, in order to absorb all the rules of the game and enjoy her first experience, being in that room made her feel good, for a while she didn't have to think about the world out there, about boredom, loneliness and moreover the ì inside no one could see or judge.

With an exciting push and pull, that first slot machine experience turned out to be positive with a net gain of € 20.

In fact, Iolanda was able to stop after just one hour of play, driven by that certain gain that could be enough to go home without disappointments or regrets.

So, she ran to the cashier where a kind and attractive girl exchanged the ticket-receipt where there was a € 70 credit on it (the € 50 initial investment plus the € 20 net winnings). The girl in charge of the cashier also explained to her that in the following rounds she could have collected the winnings independently by simply inserting the ticket-receipt in the modern automatic cashiers located in three points of the slot room.

After recovering from the hangover of that first experience, she returned to her simple life dimension for two weeks, managing to exorcise the attacks of desire to play with only fortitude. But the temptation was too much when Iolanda got ready to reach the wellness centre of the usual shopping centre, next to the slot machines room, she already knew that that day she would have given in for the second time. She felt the perverse drive of gambling blossom within his sensitive mind and this time she wanted to indulge it, indulge in the vice again.

The thought of returning to the beauty centre to look beautiful was just a poor excuse, it was just a pleasant wait before being able to dive back into the slot room.

Iolanda wallowed in those thoughts while the hairdresser smoothed her hair and talked to her about this and that. Our protagonist was already fantasizing about the possibility of obtaining the combination to access the mysterious and exciting bonus of the Pharaoh Ra's Egypt books, the previous time in fact she had not been able to try it, preferring to retire with her small but safe loot of € 20.

Who knows what fun effects would appear on the screen, and who knows what rich combinations could positively surprise her. And even if she had lost money, why would she be so bored in the face of this exciting new entertainment?

Iolanda counted the minutes that separated her from the usual coffee to be enjoyed in the bar opposite the slot room, which would also have given her the right energy to face that second gaming session that had been waiting for two weeks.

"Miss Iolanda looks really good with this coppery red"

Complimented the hairdresser on duty while Iolanda was already near the cashier to pay the bill and free herself.

"Thanks to you, as always for the welcome and for the cuddles."

Iolanda replied as she leafed through her euro banknotes to pay the bill, plus a tip for the girls who had taken care of her. After the greeting, a few more steps to the bar where this time she ordered a cappuccino, obviously observing with the corner of her eye the entrance to her slot harem ready to welcome her.

And so, while drinking his sweet cappuccino, she was already fantasizing about the number of people there could be inside the room, and then whether her favourite slot machine she had played the previous time was available again.

You know sometimes it is not just a matter of choosing any machine, sometimes you explore the slot room by calculating the positions where you are more relaxed, or where someone has spent a lot of money and then got nothing back. So, you can turn into vultures (when after noticing the prolonged defeat of some player you run to play in his slot machine hoping for a quick "robbery"), or into sheep (when you insist on playing where you are not getting a penny), or in wolves (when you win by hitting the perfect slot). Slot machines are played in a parallel dimension, in the world seen by each player, out of all the rest and obviously hoping to win abundantly.

Iolanda was excited by the idea of having to try to multiply her initial investment, trying to get great scores, bonuses or maybe jackpots that would lead her to unprecedented gains.

It was just after six in the evening and Iolanda had no plans for the evening, not even the need to have dinner after drinking that caloric cappuccino with sugar and powdered chocolate. She placed her bag in the space that divided her slot from the next one and sat in the comfortable player's chair, put in the first € 50 banknote and started. She did not win anything for all the first € 50 which disappeared in no time leaving her stunned.

Last time, at least, she had seen some good combinations, but this time it was incredible, so she tried with another € 50. The bet on each single play was € 1, so obviously in case of prolonged failure it was really easy and fast to burn € 50. After another thirty spins the slot machine continued to pay nothing and Iolanda felt a mix of disappointment and bitterness, however something prompted her not to give up. Another two € 20 bills with the playing time that had reached 2 hours, and here is the miracle that awaited the first gamble in that machine, that is, she had obtained the bonus!

Finally, the three magical books had appeared that opened the doors to the bonus game.

When the symbol of the book appeared on one of the five reels of the slot, the same emitted a jingle (sound) that created an intense suspense, the breath remains in the throat and the hope gallops, but what a disappointment if only two out of three appear.

And what an incredible satisfaction if you get even four or five. But for Iolanda three were more than enough and after such a long wait the adrenaline rush was strong, only slightly anesthetized by the regret of having had to invest a good €140 in total before obtaining them. Now she just had to take a deep breath and pray for a generous payment.

But damn, it was an overall disappointing bonus session as the total payment was only € 36, leaving Iolanda in despair with a total deficit that remained of € 104. It was enough for that day, as her head was heavy, her eyes burned slightly from fatigue and those two hours of play more than enough as a second experience. So, she was satisfied with having reduced the initial loss, collected her ticket-receipt, and went home.

After a quick shower she lay down and slept heavily.
The days following that second contrasting experience (light for the emotions of the wait and the hopes matured with the bonus, dark for the final loss) passed in the usual manner for Iolanda. Usual laziness, loneliness, the same tasks like: cleaning the house, cooking something and taking care of cats, the same reading or TV series during the evening, but this time there was that new careful thought.

Iolanda felt frequent bursts of attraction with the thought of going back to the slot room to try again, the thought of the probability of getting new bonus sessions, of seeing the total shot up on the screen, of hearing those glorious songs that the machine plays only in case of higher winnings.

On that very comfortable chair, with some coffee or prosecco kindly offered by the cashier girl inside the slot room. Obviously, the slot rooms that many people consider as pure squalor, deeply like others, who are looking for a satisfying isolation, to fill the time that is detached from the heavy routine rules that today's societies impose, or perhaps to loneliness, or for the end of a love from which you want to stay away, etc. etc.

For a person predisposed to gambling like Iolanda, two sessions alone are not enough and the search for the pleasure released by the winnings will lead her to play habitually. At that point, two possibilities will open up, the first is to play responsibly, therefore occasionally and with pre-established budgets, the second is to lose control putting your financial assets at serious risk.
Because it is well known that all addictions have something in common, and if you don't find the strength to moderate, they will win us over!

Both, alcohol, smoking and drugs, even marijuana (which in my opinion is good for health and should be legalized everywhere), if you fall into chronic daily use, any addiction will destroy us.
Without a limit in the consumption of addictive agents and without taking longer or shorter periods of pause (not to

use the bad term detox) even what makes us feel good in the short term, will end up hurting us a lot in the medium to long term. There are always exceptions to this world and some shrewd player can get lucky and the ability to better manage their relationship with gambling, creating even a fixed entry.

Think for example of the professional Texas poker players who manage to earn large sums in international tournaments of various kinds, or of the financial millionaire traders, but obviously the audience of these risk geniuses is infinitesimal.

Those who gamble becoming addicted to it will find great difficulties in managing the disease alone and sooner or later will have to resign themselves to the idea of a clean and drastic cut, sometimes to take note of the problem itself will need the help of third parties. Only after the addiction has been admitted and a relatively long detoxification (certainly not just a week or two), the subject will eventually be able to redo a few episodes from time to time and with pre-established budgets, perhaps sharing it with a loved one who will be able to check that the addiction does not explode even stronger than before.

Because the risk of relapse is enormous, and it is much higher when one is alone away from the inquisitive eyes of a possible "controller". In any case, never be ashamed of yourself, there is always a solution for every event in this magnificent adventurous journey that is life, so you must always accept the challenges and tests that life itself playfully puts before you. Iolanda found herself home alone with her cats again, but this time with one more thought. The defeat suffered in that second game session had marked her as she was at a loss of more than € 100.

Now Iolanda was experiencing a new introspective experience, through which, she had come to the conclusion that she had a real propensity for risk.

The desire to play slot machines increased day after day a little for the challenge and a little for the adrenaline that was starting to lack. Perfectly a week later she found herself back in the slot room and decided to keep that kind of frequency. Whether she liked it or not she had already developed a kind of addiction that she tried to limit with this dating rule. In the third gaming experience Iolanda bought an exciting € 80 ticket. A week later in the fourth gaming experience she won again by getting sensationally eight bonus sessions in a row in the same machine, and the total assets were a good € 340.

After a month or so from her first game, morale was skyrocketing, as both the desire and the pleasure she had for those playful sessions in her secret gaming room were skyrocketing.
But there were aspects that our slots lady could not notice on her own, changes in her habits that were lowering her quality of life, and those fixed and morbid thoughts that

now reminded her of the habit of gambling every day. And so, came the cursed fifth and sixth day of play.

On the strength of the loot won in the fourth which healed the losses of the first two days, Iolanda lost a good € 200 in the fifth and still finished the liabilities of another € 300 in the sixth.

Now to recover all the losses that had accumulated over the last two terrible days, she decided to raise the betting limit so that she could aspire to more generous winnings in less time. Her brain had gone into loss panic, so she wanted to try again and as soon as possible, the magnificent positive chemical explosion she had experienced during a big win.

Our professor was in the midst of that perfect storm that every chronic player will have to face sooner or later.

So, she broke the strict rule of the limit of one game session per week, going for the seventh session already the next day. The emotions changed along with the fear that soared. This time Iolanda went to the place of perdition, dark in the face and very tense with well over € 500 in her wallet in case she had to fight against yet another negative day, that had to be the day of redemption and after ordering her coffee directly in slot room slipped the first € 100 banknote.

Here are the symptoms of the chronic gambler who has lost control of the situation. Analysing the latest behaviour of Iolanda we can see some eloquent things.

The first is that she had blown every rule regarding the

budget which had jumped from the initial € 50 to € 100, then from € 100 to € 200, and now in this seventh out-of-control gaming session she was ready to risk € 500. At the same time the morale was low and on that day of excesses the playing time reached an incredible record of 5 consecutive hours. From the € 500 invested she was content to go home with € 350, therefore another loss of € 150 but with still a glimmer of rationality that advises you to stop.
Now the thought of the game had really become an obsession and everything else was unimportant.

Iolanda had even forgotten to leave out food for her beloved cats during that crazy day gambling, the house was more slovenly than usual but the desire to replace the things scattered in every room was really low.

She tried to stay away for a few days from that slot room, from a loving place of potentially fruitful magical games had turned into a temple of evil. But she knew it in her heart, she had to come back soon to open a new challenge, win and fly back to the top cost what it cost. Soon the time came for the eighth session which Iolanda faced with another € 500. The stake for each spin was quite aggressive and fixed at € 2, however from time to time she dared to risk as much as € 3 or € 4 per spin, compulsive madness.

This fast-paced, forced play strategy blew her entire budget away in a couple of hours. Her head was spinning, and anxiety had taken over, for the first time since she had turned into a serial gambler, she had to go to an ATM to get more cash. On the way she was plagued by a deep sense of shame with an unmotivated terror that someone she knew might see her enter and leave that cursed slot room, after all her former co-workers as well as alumni could recognize her at any moment, there, in that famous shopping centre.

That cursed day the financial butchery continued to perpetuate itself, after another three hours of play that added up to the previous two, Iolanda found herself empty-handed, hands trembling with embarrassment and paranoia. Only after reaching home and rinsing her face did she take a deep sigh and admit to herself that she had developed an overwhelming gambling addiction.
She had burned her entire pension in two weeks.
The sense of guilt and the need to offset the dramatic economic loss pushed Iolanda to cut back on shopping at the supermarket, for example by buying cheaper canned cat food, less meat and less organic products, skipping the session at the hairdresser and avoiding other expenses. In order to stem the sense of shock and deserve a new game session as soon as possible, she tried to give up many things she usually liked to do or buy, so she had officially become a slave to gambling addiction.
Other black days, some glorious days, and more defeats, the balance became more and more dramatic and Iolanda had to think about surrender, her psycho-physical health was seriously affected. When we get to the cruelest part of

this addiction with the deepest effects unleashed on every single player told here, I prefer to cut it pretty short.

The part of the sadistic narrator fits me perfectly, but I prefer to stick to the purpose of this book, which is to be a denouncer of gambling who tries to perceive the most disparate nuances, and through these stories try to give some advice in an attempt to help those who falls victim.

Returning to Iolanda we conclude this experience by confirming to you that her loss reached € 30,000 in about a year, between tears and torments that she kept inside together with a deep depression.

But something snapped inside her one day and she resigned herself to the idea of asking for help from a former colleague of hers, a professor of psychology, who in turn recommended the Dott. Randelli, a good psychiatrist expert in the problems of pathological addiction.

The feeling between her and the doctor was good and immediately Iolanda will set meetings with the psychiatrist as a way to look inside herself deeper and figure out what really caused the urge to release so much misery, either in intention or financial.

The psychiatrist Randelli showed himself a sensitive and generous soul in listening to every detail that was part of Iolanda's life, gradually accompanying her to the exit of that terrible psychological labyrinth that the game had been for her.

After a few months from overcoming that life experience, Iolanda exorcised her plunge into gambling by organizing a meeting with her bridge friends, picking them up one by one in the car to the home of the participant who had the greatest motor problems and therefore she could not move from home. They laughed, joked, got excited, and started betting only € 10 each, which was enough for the whole evening (giving a bit of adrenaline and competition), nothing but slot machines!

The real important thing that Iolanda was able to feel again after a long time was the warmth of her friends, the protection that their company aroused, the power of friendship impossible to compare with the miserable dramatic loneliness she had felt every time she locked herself up inside that gloomy slot room. Once again, the clear proof that money cannot and never will buy disinterested friendship and the daily happiness inherent in little things, another cliché that cannot be understood until the moment in which we are not living some deep crisis on a personal level.

- 7 -

HARVEY
"THE WOLF OF WALLL STREET"

A successful manager from Silicon Valley who in the late nineties and the first decade of the 2000s had amassed a fortune thanks to the digital revolution.

Meet Harvey the charming man born in Los Angeles, with a passion for travel that has led him to visit more than 50 countries around the world. At the age of forty-five already two marriages behind him but no child, freedom and open-mindedness were the fundamental principles of his personal vision of life.

A spearhead also from a sexual point of view, the legendary Harvey loved to organize parties in modern and luxurious apartments and hotels, his guests were beautiful models and transsexuals of superfine quality with an enviable femininity.

When he talked about certain erotic games and the atmosphere of those hot contexts, his eyes were on fire with that mixture of passion and perversion that only some can recognize. A true lover of eroticism without too many taboos. Life had also given him steel health, charm, successes, which, added to the countless travels and profusion of fun, made him resemble the shrewd Leonardo di Caprio in the interpretation of "The Wolf of Wall Street".

This is how Harvey appeared in front of me, showing off his bright smile like the Joker in Batman several times that mirrored mine a little. This was roughly the description of his life that he told me step by step as we played our favourite slot machine "Lighting Link".
But a second, more detrimental and obscure part, he would later confide in me at a later time. Only after trusting my equally dazzling Italian smile a little more.

We were both at the Cosmopolitan casino in Las Vegas, and both were there for the sake of playing and detach from real life for a few days. He was one of the best gaming neighbours that could happen to me both for his frankness and for the sensitivity with which he alternated long company chats with equally long silent pauses with his gaze fixed on the monitor.
But drink after drink and episode after episode we went beyond the beautiful and exciting part of our lives, we ended up confiding in our experiences in the world of gambling, then he wanted to get rid of some nightmares of his past in the world of financial trading.
We had both had many experiences in this type of high-risk investing using online platforms, and we had both laughed

and cried and got excited by the crazy adrenaline rushes impossible to describe.

Noting my willingness to disclose my trading without shame even on the bad losses suffered, Harvey wanted to open up likewise, telling me about his worst experiences as a trader. After listening to his roller coaster experiences in that world of a few sharks and many sheep, I really felt like a beggar (beggar, a term about which I and a dear friend of mine named Bruno, love to make fun of).

I mean that at most I had earned or lost tens of thousands of Euros in a few days, our dear "Wolf" Harvey had burned even hundreds of thousands of dollars a single day, while other times he had earned whole currencies.

But here we will focus on his most damaging and self-destructive period, the one that gave me goosebumps when I was there to listen to him staring into his eyes full of a mixture of excitement, fear, madness and redemption. In a game break suitable for resting the eyes and stretching the legs, we had the idea of eating something, I proposed a slice of pizza.

So, I invited the trading genius to eat a pizza in the very famous yet only for a few "The Secret Pizza", an unmarked and hidden pizzeria by the slice, reachable from the second floor of the Cosmopolitan. To be able to get there without having been there previously it would be necessary to walk between a boutique and an Asian restaurant, so as to notice an entrance to a tunnel about fifteen meters long that will project you inside the pizzeria, a total of about fifty meters. I think that place is known mostly by word of mouth (I had learned of it thanks to the tip of an English player with whom I had exchanged a few words in the previous days). In any case, the pizza is not bad at all considering that it is American-style, however far from approaching one of the only, true, Italian ones.

Harvey talked a lot in that hour of "no play" sitting on the stools of "The Secret Pizza" and illuminated by the additional lights of an old pinball machine displayed on our right as furniture. He told me about the big profits he had earned on speculations made before the great crisis of 2008, and again about the abnormal losses that had led him to semi-depression during the 2011 crisis, when, however, the gains were much more difficult to realize.
He told me how trading is controlled and moved by groups of power that are nothing more than secret associations of investors who possess enormous liquidity, so that they can all together move the trends of any market where they fit with their enormous masses of liquid money.

The so-called "Whales".

And then again, he told me how he began to lose day after day, week after week, until he was very low on cash. Luckily, he had bought a multitude of properties and valuables during the golden years between the late nineties and the first decade of 2000.

So, he had to dispose of and liquidate a couple of luxury homes in order to get back into the trading business, but only after cleaning up, a mental cleansing that lasted a good two years.

In the period of disarray Harvey was overwhelmed by a number of disastrous events and actions that made him sink. The things he described as the most trying were the shame, the disappointment, the physical ugliness, the isolation, the use in quantities of cocaine that led him to some panic attacks accompanied by depressive periods.

He pushed away from himself a large number of fake friends, prostitutes, opportunistic acquaintances, even his own family, his ex-wives. He took a whole gap year where, traveling to Europe first and then to Asia and Australia, he reset from everything he had been in the previous decade. So, at a certain point he lifted his bottle of beer and smacked it against mine saying:

"Dear Andrea, the dirt I had to eat during 2011 was also the medicine that cleaned me from things and people that had now become unhealthy for me, too many and unmanageable all together".

He was referring to false friends, overly pretentious ex-wives, whores and drug dealers who pretended to be paid employees. All gone and all dropped to a much lower profile when Harvey faced bankruptcy followed by his personal crisis. I am sure that I have had the same experiences that my conversation partner is telling me, it comes naturally to me to nod saying that I too had experienced the same. But in living and traveling I learned that these self-centred statements are sad, not very dignified and above all useless.

There is a time to talk, one to think and one to just listen. In that context, I just gave him a pat on the back and told him that he was great, and that I really don't know what I could have done to handle such situations if I had found myself in his condition, with damaging situations of enormous economic and interpersonal value.

After all, mine were only small change compared to his, the ones I had lost during my negative experiences with financial trading, I mean, and I had never despaired greatly, but at that moment I was there listening to his story and I just wanted to give him my understanding and admiration.

Remain a spectator and not try to throw myself on stage at all costs together with the one who wanted to show me his personality as in a confessional, stripping himself of everything. So even though he had only known me for a few hours, a pure unknown slot mate.

But the highlight of the conversation was the story of his intercontinental travel as a medicine to overcome that mid-life crisis, and on this obvious topic I had to intervene by also telling him the magic that enveloped my travels in Asia.

Those journeys of change, those 7 months between December 2014 and June 2015 that marked me forever and made take a spiritual and evolutionary leap.

We shared through mutual stories that living a totally new life, unable to communicate with the people from before in the same way as before, the impossibility of loving as before even those people who adored each other.

But all this was not out of wickedness but only because at that time we had to truly be reborn, when it is only you with God. God in the new seas with the new beaches, the new mountains with the new hills nearby, all incredibly familiar even if it was the first time. that we saw that landscape and that country. The people, simple, cordial, the reflection of their availability on us, the reflection of the kindness and goodness of soul that returned to us.

We understood each other on the whole philosophical and spiritual line, and we could only share more than a shiver of goosebumps by telling us in those terms.

I realized that stripped of any competition of the ego Harvey was a great man, a positive, generous, human one of those who always smile even in times of difficulty, of those who continue to support, listen and share even when they are going through a nasty period.

And this is just my personal prose of the words I was hearing that time, over there in the Nevada desert, in that wonderful fictional city of chance, in that beautiful casino, in that box called "The Secret Pizza" where I was living a lifetime like film and I felt that my trip to Asia had given me the same things as him. Just living a life number two, inside life number one, where at times you can return, for a short time or for a long time, then that is evaluated along the way.

Being winners who know how to love and who consider life crises as blessed events, to evolve.

And then Harvey came back relaxed, relaxed and told me how by selling two very valuable properties he got back on track with the liquidity necessary to resume making good investments but with an almost totally calculated risk. And so, he resumed his life of excesses at times, but never as disastrous and extreme as before. And I know, it would be nice to keep talking about Harvey and his "wild life", however this book more than a fictional story would like to be informative and useful to empower those who are lost in this crazy world of gambling.

If I could help even one person, I would be enthusiastic, helping to look at gambling addiction as something to moderate, to correct, to stop, to slide into the reassuring bed of pleasure without excess, a possible hobby that does not become an obsession.

However, after another hour of playing side by side, Harvey and I said goodbye, it was time for me to go back to my room for a bit of rest since I had been wandering around the Cosmopolitan Casino between games for eight hours; drinks, chat, pizzas and everything I have told you so far.

With gambling addiction, everyone can react differently, infinite nuances and levels of severity of the problem, so the interpretation is up to you.

For readers who were here just out of curiosity, I ask you to trust me and read my travel and erotic stories in the future, making love with different women I met throughout my life, the incredible energy exchange of sex, perversions, too they are part of human nature.

All this in the series "Love, Sex, Awareness" which will be composed of a dozen experiences with the opposite sex lived during my travels around the world. But as far as this book is concerned, I have to deepen the theme of the pathology of risk addiction, to you the second part of "The gambler".

THE GAMBLER

SECOND PART

GAMBLER PROFILE
PSYCHOLOGY AND SOLUTIONS

- 8 -

A POTENTIAL SUBCONSCIOUS CAUSE
CHILDHOOD AND YOUR PAST

I was still a child when my Father would lock himself up in the living room or sometimes in the kitchen, in total privacy with sports newspapers in hand.

My mom ran a shop, so, she never came back before evening. He, a post office worker, could enjoy a fabulous shift that started at 7:30 in the morning and ended at around 2 in the afternoon, free on Saturdays and Sundays.

A father with few vices, since his main objectives were those related to the evolution of his family, to allow me and my 2 sisters study, buy a house guaranteeing continuity and security for the future, save as much as possible and rarely gave himself some little vacation with my mom a few kilometers from our city.

He loved to compile a weekly ticket of the Totocalcio (bets on Italian football matches) and sometimes one of the Totip (bets on Italian horse races) which in the 80s and 90s were the most famous and inflated Italian state monopoly games. In those days the multitude of gambling games of

125

today did not exist, the internet was not yet a reality nor the smartphone apps that today make everything so usable and easy.

There weren't all the lotteries and gambling games of our time: Superenalotto, Winforlife , Scratch and Win, online sports betting, online financial trading, etc.

I was a child who loved football and often sat down at his side to draw up the best prediction up together for the following Sunday.

It was fun to observe the detail, the statistics, the injured players, the so-called "black beasts" (i.e some teams that on average always beat the same opponents if they faced them, their favourite victims), and anything else useful to analyse. It was above all a sacred moment between father and son where we could immerse ourselves in our world of predictions and statistics, even having a snack together.

Then when Sunday came with it, excitement and suspense came with the results that came out gradually. And off to listen to the car radio with the windows or doors open, parked near a park.

Between the first and second half an apple, a pack of crackers and a drink. So, my dear father and I often went around the city and visited his favourite bars or bookstores. You know superstition is an important factor for most gamblers: there was the bar where in the past you had already won, which was the first choice, then there was the bar where you made an attempt but then you never came back because the bartender talked too much and even looked too much, judging your compilation and your choices.

Well, no! It was not good because his observations and his look on our sacred ticket was bad luck!

In addition to the bar and betting shops my father had a couple of friends with whom he played "in company". This term means that by combining the capital, he and his "partners" could count on a larger budget and therefore increase the chances of winning, covering a greater number of predictions.

So sometimes we would go to find Oreste, a very good man who carried out his job as a shoemaker in our neighbourhood.

Or you would go to "Gianlucone il Parruccone", so called because he was perhaps more than six feet tall, slender, with a not indifferent mass of black hair.

When my father was passionately confronted with his "partners" I wandered around Oreste's shop or I wandered around the garden of Gianlucone 's house.

Sometimes the situations were reversed, that is, I wandered in the square adjacent to Oreste's shop or I sat on the sofa in Gianlucone's living room watching TV.

In our afternoons between father and son it also happened that we went to the games room, which, to be clear, were not real betting rooms as today, in Italy in the 80's and 90's there were no slots and bingo areas but only video games were played.

Then in the mid 90's they introduced the first slot machines but on which you could only play tokens, in an attempt to win others. At the limit, in the case of large victories, the "black" tokens were resold to other fellow players by applying an advantageous price to the token (compared to the price at the cashier), or material prizes were taken by exchanging the tokens directly at the cash desk in the games room. Speaking of the arcade environment, which once did not cover the role of "casino" as today, I want to tell you an anecdote that highlights the value of friendship, especially the one that is developed in childhood and that can last forever.

The pure innocence of children in contrast to the depraved money and the associated pathological vices that will never be able to compete with the human relationships between people of heart that are consolidated over time.

MY SHOCK AT THAT "FRIENDLY" REFUSAL

Many Sundays after the ritual of morning mass and the lavish family lunch that followed, my father complied with my pedantic requests to go for a "ride" to the arcade. I could hypnotize them in front of my favourite video games, meet friends and he wasn't too bored. Sometimes he sat beside me watching me play amused and other times he chatted with the other fathers sitting on the sofas in the dining area, waiting for the children to let off steam. The "Central Park" games room in Rimini which in the following years will become the fixed meeting place for myself and for many of the historical friends I still meet with today.

I cannot remember exactly how old I was, but I can surely remember, vividly, the anecdote because it's the imprinted in my memory as something of a shock

All of you will have some memories that have become fixed in childhood, while many other things you just cannot exclude from the windings of the mind.

Whenever we remember an event that happened many years ago it is always because of its weight, whether it is negative or positive. So that Sunday afternoon I had just entered the games room holding the hand of my dear father Vittorio and we were heading towards the automatic popcorn machine. He baked them in three minutes, and they could be salted or sweetened at the counter where a tray with 2 glass containers was set up on the right, one for sugar and one for salt. Not even the time to insert the 500 lire to start the automatic cooking that I was stunned by the exuberant arrival of one of my dearest friends, sensitive as well as particular ones that I still frequent today with respect and deep confidence. One of those who can keep secrets or advise on rather private or sometimes embarrassing arguments.

A toothy smile, an overflowing energy and that need for immediate physical contact were its most typical characteristics. And that day the impact was so exuberant that it physically moved me a good meter, his hand grabbed my left shoulder and he exclaimed:

"There's Andrea, there's Andrea!"

And I with my equally wide and pleased smile:

"Grande Casali! Hello." (calling him by surname)

And so far, it was all normal for me, obviously I was happy for his presence and for the fact that we could share our imaginative travels together by running around the arcade and participating in the challenges "in double".

I sacrificed popcorn when he appeared, perhaps it is better to say that I just forgot to buy them. But what dear Alberto was about to give up was so striking that it shocked me, remaining indelible in my memory and becoming our "battle anecdote" when we remember the events of childhood.

Here's how it went: After the greeting described above, Alberto's father promptly intervened and with his shrill voice he asked his son:

"Alberto buy some of those chips so you can play together right? Keep the money!".

By offering his son a five thousand lire banknote that at the time could yield a good handful of tokens:

"No dad, I don't need it, my friend Andrea has just arrived!... Let's go Andrea!".

Little Casali answered firmly without opening up to any possibility of reply. He continued to hold me by the arm pushing me towards the juke box area, also equipped with some L- shaped sofas where you could relax listening to the music offered by anyone who wanted to share it.
What we did next or what other direction we took I just can't remember but the shock of the refusal of the money and tokens was what my memory fixed around.
During all this my father was only a sly spectator.

This anecdote dating back at least 30 years ago still reminds me of the value of friendship today. The joy of a child in seeing a dear friend again, so no tokens or other money were needed to seal the meeting, the happiness of that time to spend together with the imagination was enough to fly for fun. The shock of the time was precisely in the fact that Alberto had refused precious tokens just to share time with me, incredibly without even thinking that we could invest them in a few games, commenting on their adventures. He wanted to talk face to face about something real and related to everyday life, maybe talk about cartoons, about school or about mutual friends.

I let him talk for a while and obviously I didn't blame him because even though he was a child I understood the value of that gesture. Those tokens so coveted that it was often difficult to unstitch their respective fathers, tired of spending several times for something as futile as investing in video games.

Damn, how much I had to insist at times to make him buy them, especially for the second time in the same day.

Never, ever in my young career as a video game player would I have allowed myself to refuse such a proposal from my father, especially if he had done it as an act of courtesy towards a friend. Indeed, it could be a wonderful lever to obtain them, yet Alberto had not exploited it. In short, friendship has no time, no age and above all it is not based on the material value of things.

Materialism that today gets an inconceivably important role in the scale of values, becoming one of the social cancers of the third millennium and the source of many pathologies like the one we are addressing in this book.

FROM CHILDHOOD TO ADOLESCENCE
WHEN THE VICE OF GAMBLING CONQUERS US

I hope I have not bored you with this personal story, but it was essential to make you glimpse the focal point of this eighth chapter. That is, all those days spent at the age of 7-13 had made me a potential gambler because when you are a child you absorb concepts and habits like sponges. I absolutely don't want to blame my father who is an incredible man to me; he certainly made his mistakes in carrying out the difficult task of parenting, but he never made me miss anything and he was very affectionate, of a rare goodness to find, and today I continue to love him with all my heart.

But for consistency I must admit that the activities carried out, and the time spent with him, were determining factors in my sensitive process of maturation and transition from childhood to adolescence. And so, from the age of 14/15 I began to be attracted to gambling with intensity. I played poker with friends, albeit a few lire just to create a bit of adrenaline, then I frequented the games room near my home almost every day, which was also the meeting point with all my friends. So, I was playing video games and slot machines frequently. After the age of 21, I started doing several leisure trips because I loved investing my first salaries earned in trips mainly abroad. Often when and an international city was equipped with a casino it was my duty to pay a visit, so my first experience in a real casino was in Prague between Christmas and the New Year of 1999, then Las Vegas in 2004 and Amsterdam in 2011. After these experiences Macau arrived and again Las Vegas twice.

Sometimes I won and sometimes I lost but surely the outcome tended to be negative as my visits to those realms increased, at least since the overall trip was quite expensive. But then there are those who spend on designer clothes, some on cars, some on jewellery or drugs, I spent my extra money with what I enjoyed - travel, sex and some gambling sessions.

Returning to the initial discourse then I passed from the pool cards to the arcades, from poker with friends to the casino, up to financial trading, I can say that I had developed a sort of adrenaline addiction to risk, albeit a controllable one. I do not want to go from being a strong hero and diminish my faults dear readers, however I must admit that despite playing often I have never fallen so low as to ruin my life or create serious financial problems for myself or my family.
Certainly, if I had avoided these environments, I would probably have the largest bank account, but I am firmly convinced that money does not bring full happiness.

Trust me when I tell you here that it was very hard to write this book which is not even that long, and do you know why? Precisely because laziness, the vices of life, and the use of free time in many fictitious situations, have often slowed me down.

It is not easy to find inspiration and above all to sacrifice oneself in using the brain thoroughly to create something that is at least decent to be subjected to the reading of other human beings. But for me this little book, the first ever written in my life, is a source of great pride, it is something that I completed thinking I could help someone who feels lonely and stuck in this addiction of the future.

So even in moments of intense idleness and evident addiction to gambling, every holy time where I seemed to have hit rock bottom even losing considerable amounts, I managed to clean myself up for more or less long periods. Terrible have you thought? I used the word "clean up", yes, because gambling addiction is a drug in all respects. After being back on track, over and over, again, the habit of gambling has always chased me until I am fascinated again, but today it happens with awareness and with no sur-passable limits.

As I anticipated in the previous chapter, I consider gambling addiction to be a real pathology that acts on the same chemical and cerebral receptors where drugs of any other nature intervene. Excuse me if I will be repetitive by reiterating the concept several times during this reading.

To conclude, I bring your attention back to the focal point of the first analysis, that is, the importance of your childhood and therefore of your past.

Daily habits, places you go to, and even your parents, and siblings, and friends, all have influenced our way of thinking and the way we are.

Gambling often arises from behaviours and teachings that have been nurtured in us especially during a young age. I say this to introduce you to the next chapter which is perfectly connected to what has just been written, or the discomfort of not feeling rich enough if you come from families with medium-low financial possibilities.

Either the feeling of inadequacy for past failures, or the frustration that has arisen from the reproaches suffered by your loved ones, and thus the emergence of that tendency to isolate yourself and harm yourself as self-punishment.

The awe and appeal of money obviously takes hold on those who do not have it in large quantities and exposes the risk of believing that there are easy and fast ways to earn it. But we cannot remain children or adolescents for life. The first job to do is take note reminding us that the past is past, that we cannot download the blame on other people or on old experiences.

We have to think of the present as if life had just begun, enough conditioning and just continuing to follow the old mistakes otherwise the vortex of negative habits will keep us trapped indefinitely.

- 9 -

THE SOCIETY AND THE "SYSTEM"
THE HIDDEN ENEMIES

In the previous chapter we talked about the hidden influences that come from our past, especially from that childhood which was a yard stick of the evolution of our future life. It's very important to consider the psychological pressure to which we are subjected by the demands of family, society and the system of things at all levels.

The evolution of humanity and therefore of the human being is rapid and shocking, its reflection is clearly visible for example in the technological evolution that is advancing more and more rapidly from decade to decade.

Well-being has gradually developed a society where the superfluous has become necessary. Consumerism would like to impose ever more aristocratic standards of living on us and many people in the face of this competition fall into suffering or live in the company of chronic stress.

The syndrome of not feeling up to the standards around.

Evolution does not always mean progress and we know this well, a discourse that can be extended to all areas of humanity. Today the competition between human beings is very strong, as we have just said, appearing and therefore demonstrating are more important than values such as humility and sharing.

This creates a strong psychological pressure on individuals and subjects them to a judgment that is not always sustainable. Someone is brought to live in this extremely competitive social context and manages to excel, however most people are starting to suffer from the system of excesses by developing countless pathologies also related to addictions, such as depression.

PROFILE OF TYPICAL PLAYERS AND EXTERNAL PRESSURES

The suffering that such "pressures" can give is more marked on sensitive or hypersensitive people. It seems paradoxical but the player, especially the loser, often has a hypersensitive, good and generous personality.

He tends to internalize his problems, his fears and insecurities, finding great difficulties in opening up to his neighbour. This does not mean that we cannot find gamblers with a strong personality and arrogance, but even these subjects becoming slaves to gambling can manifest problems of balance in the personality.

In search of adrenaline and new strong emotions they will risk a lot and challenge fate to the death (obviously in a metaphorical sense, at least hopefully), and in case of loss they will raise the challenge again and again, they want to win! And so, the gamblers both good & passive and bad & aggressive, will forever continue to live in a world of conflict with the chasm of total loss wide open before them. As mentioned, there is also some geniuses of gambling, poker or financial trading who manage to make a profit and live lavishly thanks to these activities without suffering any consequences.

It is obvious that there are also geniuses in this field, or professionals of self-control and statistics.

However, we are not here to praise that 1% of professional winners as they have a personality and a history totally different from those of the weakest subjects for whom we want to find remedies and solutions in spite of addiction. We said that even family and friends without wanting it directly (at least that's what we hope) can put us under pressure and feed states of insecurity and discomfort that sometimes find an outlet in gambling and risk in a broader sense. Parents often do not bless the choices made by their children as they are inclined to educate in a severe way with the aim of making them achieve concrete results. They rarely take care to understand what personal and real talents may be, the inner nuances of their children that are reflected in their dreams.

Parents create pressure in an attempt to push us to excel in life by following a primal instinct adopted to make offspring strong and competitive along the journey of life. Sometimes the parents are absent and uneducated, in this case it changes little since the lack of reference points and education are another trigger for self-harm, the lack of rules that opens a highway towards addictions.

So, whether our parents have been great educators forcing us to follow strict rules but often in disagreement with our real wishes, or whether they have been dis-educational and often at odds with each other (fathers and mothers with opposite ideas), in any case it is us and only we are the architects of our present and our future. Or at least we should think in this way, we cannot do victimization and therefore self-harm. Because in reality we are born free and with absolute freedom we should express ourselves and our abilities, however this attitude receives interference not only from parents who try to educate us better, but also from the institutions and communication systems active around us.

Directly or indirectly, they try to impose on us their way and their truths that cannot always match our true nature, because we are not standardized human beings, we are not submissive robots as many institutional powers would like to see us.

Friends are another point of reference no less important than family and may have a very strong influence especially during adolescence.

How many times do you hear about the first cigarette smoked in the company of the friend who offered it in search of complicity?

Ditto for drugs, ditto for alcohol, ditto for gambling. As we said above, a particular environment with particular friends are factors that can lead us to take the first steps towards harmful experiences or habits, so they could be the first way to learn about gambling. Then we can also create murky neighbourhood relationships with other gamblers that make us feel "less wrong".

I still remember the grim faces of those who played slot machines next to me, in the betting rooms of the "small arcades town". I remember the squalid jokes between one "episode" and another one, followed by long silences or sudden hateful curses against the machine.

For example: "What a shitty machine doesn't pay a cent! Even today it fucked me € 200 in an hour".

And when someone nearby could enjoy a hefty win, all the other envious players called "owls" would gnaw with their heads down, cursing themselves for choosing the wrong slot machine. That atmosphere in the betting rooms or slot rooms is sadly current, many will know what I'm talking about.

We really get the sodden and miserable environment that we deserve? Is it in these smoky and squalid arcades or casinos that we want to spend our precious time and money? So sometimes the behaviours of family, friends and acquaintances influence us while not being intentionally in bad faith. However, it is as if we were looking in the mirror, when we find ourselves inside a gloomy betting room with other elements similar to us, like sharing our inner ghosts in a room that makes everything less lonely and demeaning.

Like saying " well I'm not the only one to gamble so that's okay!", "I'm not the only one to bet every week on football match predictions so I'm fine!".

It's a social convention, so everyone is playing now!
It is here that even the state with its laws that should always defend its citizens, becomes both victim and executioner.

Victim for the great social damage it entails and for the huge health costs that gambling addiction causes like any other addiction to fight, and executioner because he himself is the promoter of these legalized drugs.

If one wanted to live in a coherent society then it would be better to legalize marijuana rather than gambling or alcohol, which causes incalculable social damage.

THE VICIOUS CIRCLE
THE TRANSITION FROM LIGHT
TO HEAVY PLAYER

Here is an example of how some environments or situations can become the antechamber of a gaming disease. Today games such as Fantasy Football are very popular, where you improvise as coaches and compete with a close circle of friends, generally from 6 competitors upwards. Obviously, to make the game exciting and challenging, a participation fee is often introduced, otherwise what excitement if the fight ends without a winner receiving a cash prize? Some groups play with € 50 each, someone with € 100 each and so on.

There would be nothing wrong with it as it is a one-time risk, and the investment covers a full year of play.

Unfortunately, in these game groups among football fans the desire to bet on the events that occur during individual matches also develops.

Bet on the exact results of the matches, bet on the number of goals scored, on which player will score first, on how many corners will be awarded to that team or on a series of many other combinations that betting companies have invented in the course of the last years.

We start from Fantasy Football then we share the predictions on the matches of the weekend and gradually spend more and more considerable amounts on bets.

The gambling drug does not give a chance and as the accumulated losses increase, the stakes also increase, in the famous attempt to recover the regressed losses.

You start by betting a little just for the thrill of trying, but then the situation evolves and can get out of hand.

In the event of repeated losses, the psyche, which is rather demanding, as fascinating as it is perverse, will send stronger and stronger signals of revenge.

The feelings of annoyance and profound discomfort that we feel at each loss will want to be replaced by feelings of pleasure obtainable only with subsequent victories. A vicious circle opens up that inevitably leads to the prison of addiction.

The moment we win, a second trap is triggered, because feeling proud and capable we will aim more heavily, until we fall back into the vicious circle of serial losses.

We're screwed, the deadly loop has begun.

Basically, it is just as you have just read: whether we start with a defeat or a victory if we are not skilled in self-control, in the moderation of budgets and plays, we will end up losing large sums. Anyone predisposed to become addicted to gambling in these social situations can become a slave to it in no time at all.

FEW "WOLVES" BUT MANY "SHEEP"

A very useful question these days is this: how can we live peacefully in this consumerist society if we are not rich? Almost everyone loves and wants money, designer clothes, the powerful car, the latest generation smartphone, the bottle of champagne to open in the disco, the VIP holiday in the Caribbean islands, lots of cash to spend. We could define these desires as legitimate and human in our time, but isn't it stupid to rely on gambling for easy money?

After all, is clear that for the majority of gamblers the only achievable result will be financial and psychological self-destruction. Even the financial trading that today is cleared through customs and advertised as an easy way to make money in a very short time, hides enormous pitfalls and the percentage of winners in the presence of the losers is really low, as we said every 100 sheep there is a wolf.

We can therefore say that on average 99 inexperienced players will systematically lose, while a successful financial trader who knows very well the hysterical trends of the markets, will earn large sums.

Becoming a slave to the rules of this modern society can be really easy and not only from the philosophical point of view and compliance with the rules, but you become a slave even when you are a victim of the "system" where the "wolf eats the sheep".

The poor thus become poorer and poorer, the very victim of his ignorance, and the rich ever richer strong in his dominant position.

The holder of power will live in ever more extreme ease in spite of the weak losers, because it is the financial capitalist himself who moves the market.

Whoever holds 90% of the world's capital will sell or buy assets of all sorts, deciding the movements of the markets and obviously milking the remaining cash injected by poor "followers" (pursuers without bases or skills, not in possession of secret or anticipated news that they possess the great manoeuvres of the global economic system).

Obviously, there are also good investments with miraculous returns, but they are single success stories where investors have chosen the right reality, a real company that has been successful.

Think about who bought the Amazon shares for $ 1 and today finds himself with his initial investment multiplied by 2000. Yes, because today Amazon shares are worth around $ 2000 each. Isn't it healthier and more productive to be in the reassuring and exciting world of "no risk"? Be independent and free. Maybe we won't be filthy rich, but we can enjoy an aperitif with friends instead of spending the € 50 banknote in the slot machine in sad solitude, nervously smoking 20 cigarettes in 2 hours.

Or maybe we could enjoy a nice weekend in the mountains instead of burning € 250 in a few hours on an online trading platform. And why not, go to the stadium to enjoy the exciting match of the favourite team, instead of burning € 150 in bets to be followed sedentarily on the sofa.

Maybe we will be free and happy to live a real life and not a virtual one.

THE DAMAGE OF CONSTRAINTS
YOU HAVE TO MAKE MONEY!
SO YOU WON'T MAKE ANY MONEY

Our subconscious is always working, whether we like it or not, trying to neutralize the instincts connected to our earthly ambitions that dry us out. We must always remember that we are human beings, and our DNA contains a great desire for simplicity, for contact with nature, for working in a group with other human beings and for being loved.

But as we have already said, society and today's status symbols put us under stress and turn us off, this is because it is not possible that each of us is led to mere productivity, to the mere achievement of goals and economic results, or to the appearance at any cost in perennial competition with other human beings.

And so, the cursed need to make money and satisfy the countless futile needs of modern times can throw us into the vicious circles of illusions. But the purest and most profound part that is enclosed in our mind or rather in our soul, will refuse to pursue such miserable and meaningless goals. By the time we enter the fever of gambling or financial speculation we will empty ourselves and continue to empty ourselves more and more, we will hate the same money and become less and less effective in trying to make it. It occurs to me that not even the stupidest animal on the face of the Earth would lose the freedom and abundance that life itself offers on this planet, just by trying to have more than it is allowed, all without doing. nothing.

True freedom and true abundance will come when we ourselves humans endowed with supreme intelligence and infinite mental power, change in better.

When we decide that the situations around us make us unhappy and then we will do something to root out the causes of that unhappiness. Not self-destructing.

MY EXPERIENCE
WINNING TRADER OR DESTROYER

I still remember when I started doing financial trading in 2013. In the first year I was just a novice, so I worked carefully and sparingly because I knew I didn't have all the knowledge and skills to be able to make a profit.

I won little and I lost a lot, but the losses were small and therefore psychologically not very influential.

Then after several readings, technical insights, market analysis and industry tricks, I began to grow my capital by creating a real monthly salary.

Wow I was really proud of myself and started thinking it could be the turning point in my life; perhaps from then on, I could travel around the world and be truly free by operating on the online trading platforms with the help of only my laptop and smartphone.

Besides, one of the advertising used by the same online trading platforms insisted that recently, I, as a trader, earn a huge salary working from home or traveling with a laptop, with the help of the mobile phone. I still did not realise that soon I would enter a vicious circle where tense nerves and despair would alternate several times, with few moments of success and happiness.

Yes, because the more money I made, the more I wanted without even enjoying the beautiful sums won.

I couldn't satisfy myself, but I always wanted more and therefore my playing strategies became more and more aggressive. But by the time the losses came it was very hard to digest, so I doubled the venture capital in an attempt to cover them and also cash in the missed profit on previous bets It was the nightmare of doubles, X4s, X8s, and systematically this happened in periods where the market was so unstable as to be dramatically unpredictable.

When defeats followed and undermined my financial security, every subsequent trading action I took turned out to be the wrong one, as if I was no longer able to do that job overnight. The reason was very simple, I was no longer operating with care and calm, but I was relentless on the riskiest strategies possible to try to recover the losses or maybe to quickly grind big profits.

Do you know when a tire is punctured?
Initially you continue to go with some confidence, then if you continue while maintaining a high speed the tire will blow, the rim will begin to bend and then you will reach the total destruction of the wheel with the block of the vehicle. If you are no longer able to operate with detachment and lucidity, calmly and taking restorative breaks, waiting for the favourable events that always arrive sooner or later, then the winning rhythm and self-control will be destroyed. We will lose several times.

The nervous system will be attacked by ever greater fears and insecurities, depressive states, unhappiness and fixation for those goals not achieved as intended, or not achieved at all. I was very skilled in covering up negative moods because I have always been a boy who did not want to weigh on others and who always took life with lightness and healthy madness. I am a good counsellor and psychologist when it comes to listening and advising others, but unable to seek advice or help from third parties in matters concerning me personally.

When I lost my mind, feelings of guilt crowded, the perception of failure and uselessness, after all, all the time invested was also a serious loss, in addition to the economic one. Hating these states and failing my stable and winning side, my inner voice meant enough!

There have been many moments in which I analysed myself in an attempt to understand the causes of my desire to make money, and at the same time of the madness that led me to lose even large sums.

Then maybe I would win again, and my morale would go back to the top, so I realized I was addicted to some kind of drug, the excitement of the roller coaster of emotions that gave me the risk. They made me a bit of a warrior and a bit masochistic. Sometimes I would go into crisis and seriously lose until I found the last money of desperation on the gaming (or trading) account. In those moments I felt a kind of perverse sense of self-protection arise within me, I mean that I was aware of the fact that now I could no longer recover my losses with that small residual capital, but I was willing to play that too instead of saving it.

At that point of the crime, I preferred to destroy myself completely to definitively end with that sort of addiction and hope. Losing everything to be free! I remember many times when the account on the trading platform ended inexorably at zero, even losing € 4,000 or € 5,000 in a few hours driven by the crazy attempt to double them.
What a rush of adrenaline, but 70% of the time the outcome was negative, only rarely did I bring home miraculous doubling of the capital. And then when the account finally marked zero and I could no longer replenish it because I lacked liquidity, a feeling of well-being and freedom ensued. Self-destruction was sometimes the only way out of that state of full dependence, self-destruction and total loss as acts of liberation.

I have just described with no small difficulty the perverse addiction that can reduce players to real masochists.

RISKING ALL JUMPING WITHOUT A PARACHUTE

The serious problem of gambling and financial trading comes from the fact that many of the people who practice today cannot afford it. Poverty and hardships push more and more people to gamble in the hope of making money miraculously, this is impossible!

The online gambling websites themselves or their media advertisements state "play responsibly" or "invest only as much as possible, in relation to your financial status".

However, these clichés remain only good advice from the bodies responsible for controlling the game, posters to wash one's conscience, the same for those written in such small characters as to be difficult to read, on the periphery of the web pages of betting sites.

The truth is that psychologically weaker players will end up desperate in their loneliness and first squander their already meagre finances. We reiterate that pathological gambling creates serious social damage, and the state should be aware of this. Other people will find these speeches exaggerated. However, I reiterate that the content of this book is meant to be a tool to give strength and hope to those who are victims of it.

All can be resolved. Strength and Courage!

- 11 -

THE ORGASM OF DEFEAT
ENJOYING WHEN YOU LOSE

The title of this chapter is paradoxical, but I am sure you will be able to understand its meaning along the way. I just talked about "player masochism" that will tend towards financial self-destruction in a sub-conscious attempt to end the addiction that has become his trap. The perversion of the human mind is well known and manifests itself in various spheres of the personality, so when gambling becomes chronic in a pathology that is no longer manageable by the individual gambler, he could lose touch with reality.

In the new distorted reality, the same desperate player could become a " systematic loser ", that is a person no longer able to settle for the partial winnings that he will get following the previous losses, thus ending up destroying even the positive results. Any new winnings will never seem enough when taken individually, as the player's goal remains to recover all previous losses. So, if today he wins €150 in the presence of a total accumulated loss of € 1000 over time, he will continue to risk those €150 just won. The wisest thing would obviously be to set aside the € 150 and try again at a later time, with greater clarity and a rested mind. Or in the case of financial trading, when the market will repeat a favourable trend.

This would be a healthy and intelligent reasoning which, however, cannot be contemplated when discomfort causes the gambler to lose control.

So, when the initially invested capital is seriously damaged, the pathological gambler or trader will carry out high risk operations, in an attempt to wash away the losses and the sense of guilt and unhappiness connected to them, thus leading to exhaustion day after day. total of its financial resources.

THE LAST DESPERATE ATTEMPTS

The chronic player (for example from slot machines) who has already lost large sums will gradually raise his target of satisfaction to be achieved. Any winnings obtained will be reinvested in the utopian dream of recovering all the stolen goods. If he wins a jackpot or important figures he will run to play again in the following days or weeks with the risk of losing even these newly obtained winnings that are not enough (for example) to cover the accumulated losses.

The only way to get out of the nightmare of this loop of the game could probably be to get a win big enough to zero all the losses accrued, and possibly an additional profit.
But in real reality, and not distorted by the chronic player's dreams, how many times can such a large fortune ever happen in statistical terms? Perhaps only one person in 100,000, just think of the various jackpots of lotteries or casinos that are paid rarely and very few lucky subjects (when compared to the mass of suitors who play daily).

Both the victims of addiction who will be sadly nodding in their hearts, and the readers who are not addicted to gambling, all can see the great stupidity of those who delude themselves to make money through gambling. So, with the terms "masochistic player" and "financial self-destruction" I describe those people who have become so much slaves to pursue a reckless lucrative plan thanks to gambling. Consequently, the compulsive actions that the gambler carries out in the attempt to resurrect himself will lead him to the definitive drying up of the available liquidity.

This is why in the gamblers we can identify the unconscious, perverse, with detrimental behaviours, such as those of continuing to invest the small sums left feeling the peak of pleasure when these too are extinct.

Kill the cause of the pain, the money! Damn money.

It is an unconscious system of self-defence, in fact the brain that can be our ally as well as our dangerous adviser.

So, perceiving that suffering repeated over time and caused by gambling, he will want to put an end to it.

The only cause that can continue to fuel this degenerative addiction - money - will have to be destroyed! We will have physically gotten rid of the "gambling addiction" problem at its root.

When the money runs out after the last desperate bet, the pathological player usually experiences two very strong and opposite feelings. On the one hand, the misery and shame for having really destroyed all his money or in any case a large sum, and on the other hand the joy of the paradoxical fact of not having more resources to invest (at least in the short term).

Now the player will be able to try to detoxify by putting an end to those terrible feelings of losing a slave to the game.

At this stage, gamblers are aware that they will soon have lost everything, even instinct tells them that it is time to wave the white flag. This is why, generally, the highest bets and capitals invested in a single game or trading session (as a percentage of the total available capital), appear to be at risk in this phase of final "desperation".

In the final phase, self-control jumps and therefore the "money management *" is no longer respected although it is an essential when trying to make money in the stormy ocean of gambling and financial gambling.

*Money management: in the world of financial investments and risk, the precautionary strategic plan which recommends investing a maximum of 2/3/5% of the entire available capital is defined as "Money Management".

For example, if we have € 1000 to invest in trading or gaming operations, we will never have to risk more than these percentages for any single financial or risk operation. In this way, in the event of a loss, we will not significantly damage the total capital and we will be able to try again to make it bear fruit in subsequent, better or more fortunate situations and conditions.

If our "money management" turns out to be 20/30/50%, a few failed operations would be enough to seriously damage our total investment capital, or completely exhaust it.

SURRENDER OR MADNESS

The phase we have just described can be very favourable for detoxification since there are no more funds available, it is a bit as if a drug addict no longer had the substance so, even if in suffering, he is forced to do it less.

Unless the player is a criminal who, in order to continue playing, commits a crime, or slips banknotes from his mother's or wife's purse, and unless the player is so involved as to ask for loans in order to risk more money, that this phase of final agony could be the right blow to try to redeem himself.

The bad feelings and situations experienced could push him towards a positive rebound. He may confide in someone for comforting help, he may decide to consult a psychologist, he may just decide to stop thinking about the game because he is too busy rebuilding his life.

Sometimes hitting the bottom even financially could become an opportunity to take in something you believe in, to change a profession, to go on an adventure abroad.

Each human being is so particular that it is impossible to describe what can happen, but certainly you can get out of the vortex of gambling even after a single traumatic experience.

Or unfortunately bounce in and out of it over and over for the rest of your life.

Or develop a certain wisdom that, mixed with a new awareness of one's limits and those attributable to luck, lead to a new management of risk. In this new life the player will know how to moderate and play just for fun in some event, with thoughtful and not too expensive plays.

- 12 -

THE CHRONIC GAMBLER PROFILE

How does the chronic gambler think? How does it relate and behave? What are the unethical actions he might take? How can it react if discovered by family members? And if he decides to give up, how can we help him?

In this chapter we analyse in detail the behavioural metamorphosis that most chronic gamers undergo as they start living in their new world, the illusory and distorting bubble of gambling addiction.

The Player: chronic gambling as the mind is the same

Chronic players actually believe they can get an income from gambling and continue to severely damage its finances. When the losses become large, he believes he can recover them by continuing to play, actually increasing the chances of losing all or almost everything. He may believe it is a matter of luck or statistics and that sooner or later the win of the century will come and save him. He believes he doesn't have a problem or in any case he can manage it and be able to get out of it independently when he wants.

He does not realize the deterioration in his quality of life and even when he does, he remains a passive victim.

For the chronic gamer, gambling comes first, he will think about it while he eats, while working, while talking to someone. He will think about it before falling asleep and immediately upon waking up. He can skip appointments and commitments to run and try his luck.

The chronic player can lose the measure of the time playing for hours and hours ignoring even the external solicitations such as calls, messages, etc. And if these arrive, he is rather annoyed.

If you are a gamer and feel that one or more side effects of gambling addiction are manifesting in you, try to rest your mind, think carefully about what you are feeling.

Then alone or confiding in one or more loved ones, try to immediately stem these symptoms of gambling or trading hangover (whatever your addiction), before becoming real zombies or slaves, isolated in your secret desperation.

The player will tend to isolate himself and protect his secret activities

The chronic player will begin to spend most of his free time in his gaming activities rather than doing other social activities and therefore in contact with others. He will use the remaining free time to rethink the game sessions carried out, or perhaps how much money he has left to spend, or how to get more money if it is finished. By isolating himself he will play alone with the constant fear of meeting someone who can recognize him by asking for explanations. He is afraid that someone will investigate his activities and discover his pathology. The chronic player often has veils of sadness, disappointment, apathy, restlessness in his eyes.

The chronic gambler lies to others

The chronic gambler will systematically lie to questions such as: where do you go every day at that time? But in the last period where are you spending all this money?
Why don't you come to the gym or play soccer anymore? What did you do with the money I lent you?
The chronic gambler, if discovered, will try in every way to reassure the querant by smiling and saying that everything is ok, that it is just a little vice or that he has already decided to quit. He will even deny the evidence and thus, if caught or pressed by suggestive questions, he may become short-tempered or aggressive.

The chronic gambler will give up many things in order to play

The chronic gambler without great financial means to invest, will begin to give up the purchase of clothes, accessories, could use a bicycle to save on petrol, will even save on food expenses, all this and more if helpful for setting aside a budget to invest in the game.
He will give up a weekend or holiday plans if he has already calculated in his mind that this budget will have to

be invested in gambling.

So, the chronic gamer could skip a meal or even sleep from a prolonged gaming session or the depressive effects caused by yet another loss. He can ignore his partner also from a sexual point of view, forget the commitments and collapse in his work productivity. He can be completely absorbed in the obsession with the game.

The extreme actions that a chronic gambler can perform

The gambler can ask for loans from friends and in case he is unable to honour them nor will he postpone the return with the most desperate excuses.

The chronic gambler can steal money secretly from family members, partner or even in the workplace if he has the opportunity to handle cash. Specifically, he could also be:

• Taking out mortgages or loans to be able to continue playing or in an attempt to cover losses. He can sell movable property, jewellery, other luxury goods in order to get the budget to invest.

• Getting to sell real estate to invest the proceeds in the game itself.

• Crime if they come from a low social class, from degraded environments or if they do not have a decent basic education.

The vices connected to gambling to which the player could give in

The chronic player can be dominated by other vices that can cheer him up during the games, actually gambling is a real drug so it could harmonize and be completed with other types of "pleasures" or addictions.

Many chronic players like to smoke cigarettes or drink alcohol thereby increasing the taste of the game.

It is very common to notice the gambler carrying a pack of cigarettes and possibly an alcoholic drink. Mints can also be important, which occasionally break the marked and persistent taste of tobacco and alcohol.

Potential compulsive actions in the chronic gambler

As already stated, when the pathology is deep and ingrained, the chronic gambler can lose control of himself and contact with reality. The most obvious context is the loss of respect for the value of money as well as the lack of respect for loved ones. It often happens that after losing all the initial budget, the chronic player runs to the ATM to make an additional withdrawal that allows him to continue pursuing the victory.

The chronic player, for example, could reserve the slot machine in which he was playing in order to return to play once the cash withdrawal has been made, with the generally illusory hope of winning on the second attempt.

Sometimes the runs to the ATM and the attempts to play can be multiple, in a few hours. Or a Texan poker player who has just left a table as a loser might run out to buy more chips and soon return to the attack with a later attempt. An online financial trading player, as soon as the account on the platform is drained, could order a transfer immediately, knowing that the money will take 1 to 3 working days before it can be available again on the gaming account.

So, he will suffer with the wait as the market will continue to move and he will not be able to operate until the amount ordered is credited.

These compulsive and repeated actions create serious cases of bank account dilapidation, including the commitment of all the monthly availability on the credit card. Sometimes the player can spend his entire salary on wagers just a short time after receiving it.

Behavioural changes of the chronic gambler

Already in the last paragraphs and here and there in the previous chapters we have brought out the lines of the psychological profile of a gambler who becomes chronic. However, we are not talking about the profile of a potential gambler, we are talking about the description of the behavioural changes and psychology of a player who is already obsessed with the game, already totally addicted.

So here are the behavioural changes. At any hour of the day the player can disappear without explanation if they feel inspired or can't hold back the urge to play.

He will make up excuses to cover escapes or delays.

He may decrease his appetite and eat irregularly.

He may decrease his attention to hygiene.

In the chronic player one can figure out an increase of sadness, apathy in a constant state of absence and restlessness, or on the contrary in relation to his personality he could become paranoid, aggressive or victimised.

It can develop forms of hypersensitivity towards saving, which is paradoxical, but completely explainable.

In fact, the gambler, by spending large amounts of money on gambling, instinctively tries to stop this "financial bleeding" by saving on everything else. He can become depressed and thus change his outlook on life and the world. In that case he will see most of the things that happen in a negative light, he could develop catastrophic views on the evolution of society and the world. Consequences absolutely connected to a depressive state.

The chronic player may even develop some physical alteration, with increased sweating, shaking of the hands and body, blurred or less clear vision, weight loss or weight gain. He can become sedentary by abandoning previous physical activities. As previously introduced in some extreme cases the chronic player can develop criminal instincts, steal, not honour debts or become violent.

The chronic gamer in the case of a markedly proud personality may begin to blame or blame loved ones or partners for the failures that have occurred previously or currently in his life. I am forced to list even the most extreme case of self-injurious behaviour on the part of the chronic gambler. In fact, he could even develop suicidal instincts when losing everything falls into total despair. Today we have several problems that affect society and every single individual.

From my point of view, gambling can be included in the list of psychological drugs and therefore it is a phenomenon that should not be underestimated, as the symptoms it entails are not to be taken lightly.

For this reason, if you notice one or more signs, behavioural nuances, strange actions such as those listed above, ask yourself if your partner, friend, acquaintance may have ended up in the vortex of gambling addiction.

If you yourself are a chronic gambler or are on the road to becoming one, try hard to detox, do it now.

So, we both know that this is not the right way to solve your financial problems and is much less likely to solve your unhappiness (for facts of life) that makes you to isolate yourself in this crap.

- 13 -

PROBLEMS ON YOUR
PSYCHO-PHYSICAL HEALTH

When you get trapped inside the murky world of gambling addiction (reiterating that we include betting, financial trading, casinos, slot machines, green tables and the like) your energy and health are weakened and deteriorated at all levels.

Sleepless nights, sleep to catch up and mental fatigue

The quality of sleep worsens as anxiety and a fixed thought towards the game can accompany the player even between the sheets. Many players enter the slot room in the evening and do not stop playing until closing, or in casinos that have continuous opening hours to the public, 24 hours a day, players practice at any time, sometimes losing track of time.

I also personally remember having some very long play at on online casinos directly from my computer, on those occasions I could stay up all night until I had lost everything or had not earned a satisfactory amount.

So, to catch up on sleep I lost the whole next morning by staying in bed.

I remember well these states of physical and mental fatigue that these extravagances caused me. Sometimes after losing all the budget invested, I stared at the ceiling thinking what damn profit?

It hurt even more to be aware that all that tiredness, that wasted time, that need to sleep the next day, had not even produced a return. It was truly a loss on all counts!

And the conditions were the same if it was financial trading, here too there were happy times where I won big and was satisfied, but sooner or later I would have entered a negative period that would have absorbed my energy, because this is the "out of control" gambling drug, this is the curse of greed, this is the negative energy that revolves around easy money or purported easy money.

Smoking and alcoholic companions in misfortune

It is certainly not true for all personalities who gamble, however in my case I loved to "enjoy" the games in the company of cigarettes and drinks. I have never been an alcoholic, at least this I can swear to you, but surely 3 or 4 fresh beers, vodka-tonic, alternatively whiskey or other spirits I drink them with pleasure from time to time.

As a player I would light up a cigarette at least every ten minutes that marked the pushes of a button on the slot machine, the raising of cards at poker, or the waiting time before the financial trading operations closed.

And think that today I am no longer a smoker. Just a few joints with 100% natural marijuana inside. I never missed the opportunity to light a cigarette when I obtained a bonus on the slot machine, those were really the smokes and drinks that tasted better because it accompanied a success. In practice, as you all probably know, slot machines "pay" a bonus from time to time, this gives a certain number of free spins with multipliers or other random "pluses", special prizes that can yield huge winnings.

That in my opinion is the moment when cigarettes are tastier and impossible to avoid and even if I had just put one out, even if the bonus came 2 minutes later, there I was going to light another… For heaven's sake!

I have never been a heavy smoker of those 2 packs a day, but the thrill of gambling could push me to be. The next morning, a dry throat, little coughs, even a few days of your life throw down the toilet in addition to the money you may have lost.

SEDENTARY LIFESTYLE
LAZINESS AND ISOLATION

When you have entered the tunnel of gambling addiction you are full of thoughts and a hidden smile.

There is a tendency to nourish activities that are not sensible and unhealthy to the detriment of the more virtuous ones. In times of greatest stress, you don't have the desire or the strength to go to the gym or play soccer, you prefer to stay on the sofa watching TV or wallow in sad thoughts. Even at work, every activity becomes heavy and the energy used in carrying out tasks is decidedly reduced. Same thing with regards to outings in company and meetings for recreational purposes where you have to meet people, talk or compare. It is as if you've lost contact with reality and from the classic more or less serene everyday life you entered a new world of isolation with daily activities reduced to a minimum.

Surely all this is determined by psychological factors such as guilt, shame, disappointment, and if even depression occurs.

- 14 -

HOW TO GET OUT OF GAMBLING ADDICTION OR LIMIT IT

I have reached the most difficult part to write both because I know what a challenge it is to untie yourself from the temptation of the game and because the responsibility for the advice to give you is so great. Furthermore, we human beings are always different from each other, so we cannot generalise.

But as I did from the beginning, I will simply try to recall the sensations I felt in my periods of risky activity, from which the strength to learn to manage everything arose within me. I decided to strip myself of all shame and share with you all the steps that have marked my victory against gambling addiction.

Reflecting on it, observing its effects, touching its negativity and then setting rules and conventions that have made me today's winner, both when I play and when I invest, both for pleasure and for profit. Now we reiterate the fact that gambling can be lived with, and while this statement may seem scandalous in this context, I confirm it. In fact, it is not that all people who have had serious problems or have burned through large sums, cannot continue playing from time to time. Of course, they can if they can regain control to decide when enough is enough and stifle the temptation when it arises with arrogance or too frequently.

I am an example of this since as I mentioned I continue to play poker with old friends, but again, only a few euros. In addition, I go on a whim to play at the casino once a year when I travel for pleasure to cities that have them, but with strict rules, for example having a pre-established budget to invest and time limits. It is also true that for some it is better to stop forever because they are unable to control the inner impulses that call for heavy play.

The absolute ban does not benefit everyone and is like depriving a former alcoholic of a glass of wine or a few beers every now and then following a detox.
Or is like banning a marijuana smoker from the occasional joint for relaxation just because in the past he has abused smoking marijuana every day.
We must be aware that the problem is not gambling itself or alcohol or anything else, the problem is always to keep a balance, to learn to enjoy the pleasures of life in moderation. Actually, only when we enjoy vices in moderation, we fully enjoy them, the excess nausea makes those pleasant playful moments lose their meaning. It is so even with sex!

Obviously, the vast majority of people love sex, but if it is done compulsively, extremely and obsessively, it loses its value, don't you agree?

Maybe not, but on this last example I want to give you carte blanche. It is time to give us some motivation, to push us out of the slavery of gambling addiction. I am sure that all the things you will read you already know very well.

The great effort lies in reiterating and reiterating them, reiterating them within yourselves because there is no more time to waste and it is time to love and respect yourself, your freedom and your physical and mental health can no longer wait.

Love yourself: earning costs effort

Damn how many times have I cursed myself thinking about the money burned in gambling, not because I am a stingy or a fixer, rather the opposite, but thinking about how I could have invested that money.

Think of the chronic players who go so far as to deprive themselves of new clothes, a pair of sunglasses, a dinner with friends, a pleasure trip, all because they destroyed their money on gambling without any advantageous return. Not to mention the problems that can sometimes be caused to loved ones whether they are parents or partners. I honestly would have invested the money lost in the world of risk in women, fine food and above all travel.

Not that I have missed them since I have visited around 35

countries in the world "falling in love" with more than 200 women now, but you can always do better in life.

Every day we go to work and apply our skills and our time to earn the income that allows us to live decently.
And sometimes we may even have work problems given the precariousness that characterizes today's times.
So, whether we lived in the first condition with stable work, or in the second of precarious work, in any case the damned money we get comes from the use of our time and our skills. By focusing on this aspect it will be really terrible to think about the fact that you can burn a € 50 or € 100 banknote in a few minutes. Even if we were well off and have good capital, when we have squandered all the savings, we would find ourselves desperate and in misery.

There are those who will be able to sell valuables or even a house, only because of the losses from gambling or any other form of high-risk investment; in these cases, we would have really lost the complete balance.
We can no longer be happy in simple living and we no longer believe in ourselves and in our qualities.
Having entered this vicious circle, we are willing to punish ourselves by destroying one of the things that today creates the greatest pressure on the whole of society, money.

The time has come to embrace the discipline, the same that paradoxically the chronic player engages in meticulous savings that allows him to scrape together the budget to squander in the game. We know this paradox very well and we have already introduced it in the first chapters.

The addicted player who starts saving on gasoline, clothes, shopping, the gym, dinners out, a gift he had to give to someone, a savings freak just to throw everything into the crematorium of gambling addiction.

Terrible yes! That's enough! Dear heavy player, give yourself four "slaps" on the face, look in the mirror and immediately reverse this unhealthy thought.
Save money yes, but for real life and to build or live what you really want in your life!

Love yourself: do physical activity and stay in company

Slaves of gambling addiction we isolate ourselves and become dark in the face and afflicted within, so we no longer feel up to the company of all the other people who revolve around us our daily life. Isolation as an antechamber of depression is one of the darkest aspects of gambling addiction or despair from compulsive investments, so we must realise this and file any shy attitude towards others as well as any action that leads us to loneliness.

When we can laugh and chat with the people, we love whether they are family or friends, we bring ourselves back to the warm and reassuring bed of real life, made up of emotions, sharing and love. When our mind bounces with an obsession of the vision of the slot hall or casino or trading platform, we invite a dear friend for a walk, have a drink together and talk about life.

This seems boring and worthless to us when we are in the vortex of addiction, but it is one of the keys to get out of the closed universe of the world of addictions and come back to life. Love, which is the greatest force in nature, can also help us move forward in a miraculous way. We forget too often how human beings love to listen and help. Let's ask ourselves this question! If a close friend or partner came to us at a very fragile time in their life and opened up, asked us for advice and confided to us that they have a serious problem with gambling, wouldn't we be happy to help them?

Wouldn't we feel compassionately happy and helpful to his cause? The answer is always YES! So, we must learn to give in, to abandon shame and fears and confide in our loved ones, even to those who are very intimate with us as a partner can be.

Another oxygenating and perfect action for rapid psycho-physical rehabilitation is physical activity. We prepare our sports bag and run to practice the sport we prefer, perhaps in the pleasant company of a dear friend who will motivate us. Let's go back to the gym and try to get back to the rhythms of the past, or if we didn't practice, maybe let's start now and sign up! The feeling of purification from all the waste that gambling pumps into the body will be swept away, oxygenating ourselves we will see all the stupidity that lived within us come out into the open. We will be clear and consistent, and we can begin our rebirth.

Love yourself: save part of your economic income

When we are not really able to stop destroying our money, but we are determined to get out of it, a very useful thing can be to rely on third parties. It can be a loved one or a financial advisor (if we want to remain anonymous), in any case a winning strategy is to start setting aside a percentage of our income.

We will endeavour to pay this fixed amount into some untouchable account or deposit on a regular basis, so that we will no longer have the cash we generally destroyed in the game.

For example: I undertake every month to pay 20% of my income into a blocked fund from which I will not be able to withdraw any amount until a long-term date wisely agreed with the advisor, the partner, the family member.

So, we get rid of the temptation to play every extra penny that apparently doesn't affect the normal economic needs we need. In the meantime, we will detoxify from addiction by taking action on all the other fronts that we have exposed earlier in this same chapter. The advisor will help us curb our compulsion and we will gradually feel proud of the activity of rebuilding our savings.

This person can be a stranger or a family member, the important thing is that he / she can be trusted. It would be deleterious to start this forced saving activity by relying on risky investment funds or which in turn could make us nullify every effort made in an attempt to "respect" more the value of money.

YOGA AND MEDITATION
A MIRACULOUS SUPPORT
FOR FREEDOM

Now I want to share with you this unusual topic for a context like addiction, and I'm sure someone was surprised when reading the title. However, the activities of yoga first and then meditation have helped me tremendously in every aspect of my life, especially when I was waiting for the right enlightenment before making decisions.

In the most important period of my life when I no longer loved the job I was doing and felt the need for a radical change,

I started a yoga class that I had seen advertised on the internet. I cannot explain to you what it instilled in me, the strength to react by trying this path, and I did.

The yoga class I took was the solving experience of that phase of my life. I went to the course 3 times a week, I saw new faces and savoured the kindness of the people who practiced with me, primarily the yoga teacher who is a person with incredible energy. At first it was hard to practice as yoga is a form of extreme stretching, then gradually my body became more flexible and I soon became a good practitioner. I still practice yoga alone and 7 years have now passed since that first course that restored my psycho-physical balance.

It is really true that yoga makes you flexible inside and out by moving an energy that is already inherent in us but which we never think to draw on it.

The sense of slight pain during the most extreme positions leaves room for a kind of orgasm that runs from the tip of the toes to the head, it is the energy that flows.

The vision of life becomes optimistic, the desire to love and respect each other increases exponentially, the so-called awareness explodes inside you and the curiosity towards other practices that help to personal balance pushes you to explore new ones. When I practice a yoga class, I was in fact intrigued by meditation, which I started practicing and loved in a few weeks.

It was very difficult initially to keep out of the mind the thousands of daily thoughts that crowd it, close your eyes and not think about anything, visualizing only what the infinite imagination of the soul can offer us.

Then it gradually became a journey, more and more expandable, more and more infinite.

I travelled by visualizing any terrestrial or astral paradise that was inspired by my consciousness and imaginative mind, or perhaps it is better to say, by my soul.

On this point I strongly suggest my dear readers, if you suffer from restlessness, compulsive actions and the types of addiction like these discussed here, trust your inner voice and open it with the help of yoga and meditation. Try yoga without shame, whether you are a man or a woman, you don't have to be wary or ashamed.

This activity is not tied to any religion or dogma as many thinking, is just a spiritual practice that sets you free.

It will stimulate your desire to listen to yourself, to reflect on the meaning of life, on all the miracles that happen every day and every minute around you.

What is the infinite universe made up of billions of stars out there, how does a flower or a plant grow from a small empty seed, what is wind, fire, water and every other chemical process?

What is the mission of our life? Everything will appear more magical and fantastic, and in the presence of all this wonder what are the miserable little problems of our daily life? Maybe they don't exist, we create them, so addictions are really a big bullshit, we have to think about it, laugh about it and abandon them immediately thanking them. Being thankful that we lived with all these obstacles and that pain, and the feeling that they are now only positive life experiences. Now we have grown up, now we have evolved. With every crisis in life, we need to flourish to become more beautiful and stronger than before.

ACT NOW!

Dear friends, we are really finished, and I want to leave you with my greatest good luck and with a strong hug but followed by a strong push. We are all brothers on this wonderful planet Earth and not even the impositions dictated by other human beings should frighten us or make us suspicious. We were born to be happy, to live life as a wonderful game where our mission is nothing more than to pursue dreams and carry out our tasks in the best way. Act today! Now that after reading this short book you may feel a push that comes from within you, now that you have the courage to say enough to the slavery of gambling addiction.

And this advice I give you even if you have a different problem from the one addressed here but you just found yourself reading this Kindle by chance. As on that magical day in 2013 where something prompted me to intercept the advert of that yoga class which opened the doors to an unstoppable change, so I hope this book will trigger you today. You know when you are fascinated and moved to see something artistic?

When you look at a show or a play and are excited and think "Happy Days - tomorrow I'm going to enrol in some acting classes," or when, as kids we fell in love with a sport seen for the first time and thought "this is the sport I want to practice".

Dreaming and trying is valid for anything, but you must act immediately and believe in it, because if you let the time pass, the enthusiasm will be consumed, the desire will vanish, and you will do nothing more to pursue your small or big dream, your personal revolution.

Run to confide in the person who could best listen to you and understand you without any prejudice or judgment, or from an expert in the field who can help you against this pathology! Here my task is finished, close everything and run, come on. I would be so happy if I could help any of you.

- 16 -

SOME CONCLUSIVE DATA

The profile of the problematic gambler

Through the data collected from the study and the literature, it is possible to define the profile of a problem gambler: generally, it's a male individual, with an unhealthy lifestyle that includes alcohol abuse, compulsive smoking and/or drugs, who plays mainly with slots and Vlt machines and gambles on-line

Peculiar characteristics of the problem gambler are a high sensitivity to boredom and the search for satisfying sensations, even with a high propensity to personal risk. In the most problematic cases it is also possible to find him extraneousness to the world around him, impulsiveness, inability to express and perceive emotions.

The pathological player also tends to attribute his defeat to the game to mere bad luck, while the victory is absolutely attributed to his ability as a player even in the case of games where no skill is needed.

Those who have problems with gambling also tend to go into debt to satisfy their mania. According to a survey by the Superior Institute of Public Health, 27.7 % of the players interviewed obtained loans from financial companies compared to 4% of non-players and 14.2% also requested loans from private individuals compared to 0.9 % of non-players. Another important factor is the place where you play: you prefer places far from your home or place of work and with the security of having guaranteed the privacy of your games. An element that demonstrates the perception of social shame related to the phenomenon of compulsive gambling, which makes it even more difficult to identify.

The risk of gambling addiction among young people

Although the profile analysed so far corresponds to an adult man, the phenomenon of pathological gambling among younger children shouldn't be underestimated. Research from the Superior Institute of Public Health, tells us that most of the 700,000 young players are male, from the south or from the islands and attend technical and professional institutes. According to estimates, 68,850 of them turn out to be problem gamblers.

We are talking about minors who habitually gamble and have serious problems quitting. They mainly practice sports betting (79.6%) and instant lotteries (70.1%), methods of play that are more easily accessible to them and with fewer controls by suppliers. According to the study, it is very likely that once they are 18 they will also move to other types and modes of play.

Studies carried out in the area also highlight strong critical issues regarding young people. According to a research by Caritas of Rome on a sample of 1,600 children between the ages of 13 and 17, 36.3% gamble at least once a month. The most popular games are sports betting, widespread among 88.3% of the interviewees, scratch cards, usually used by 48% of the sample, and online bets, made by 30%. The Caritas study also highlights how the main vehicles that lead young people to learn about gambling are TV commercials and online advertising.

It is likely that those who regularly follow sports on television are more sensitive to gambling advertisements that we can normally find in the interludes of a football match or any other sporting event.

In contrast to the phenomenon of excessive gambling advertising, in July 2018 the aforementioned "Dignity Decree" introduced a ban on signing new contracts for the promotion of gambling. As expected, the initiative found the unfavourable opinion of the Italian League Seria A (many professional teams are sponsored by important gaming companies) and the Italian Game System.

The illegal gambling market

Although the data of the various studies show that players are more concentrated in the center-north, it is also necessary to evaluate the substantial amount of illegal gambling present especially in the south and not recorded by the studies. It is not easy to estimate how extensive the underground economy is in the hands of mafias and organized crime.

According to some estimates by the Central Service of the Postal Police and Telecommunications, in 2015 the turnover of criminal organizations in the sector would have been 23 billion.

In some areas it is customary that the slots and Vlt machine under the control of the Monopolies are replaced with other machines modified and controlled by the local mafias. Keeping track of the bets made on these machines is impossible, unless after their seizure.

For example, in 2018 the anti-mafia of Palermo discovered that all the bets that took place in the agencies of the entrepreneur Carlo Cattaneo went to finance the inaction of the boss Matteo Messina Denaro. In addition to being leading players in entrepreneurship linked to gambling in Italy, mafia members often exploit game mechanics to launder dirty money.

For example, thanks to the Vlt machines, which allow you to insert banknotes directly, traffickers can easily clean up thousands of euros.

Gambling has therefore consolidated as a solid business also for organized crime and consequently the mafia is one of the main stakeholders in the industry.

Gambling is therefore confirmed as the most profitable social scourge of our country, to the delight of dealers, criminals and, alas, the state coffers.

Commitment of local administrations, albeit coordinated, is not sufficient to counter the phenomenon, so structural intervention by the central government is necessary.

As anticipated, the current executive has included the fight against gambling among the points of government contact even if the few initiatives implemented so far have been judged insufficient or even counterproductive even by those who oppose the slot lobby.

All that remains is to wait for the near future to understand if there will be more decisive interventions, and if the State will find the courage to give up substantial economic revenues in order to limit the spread of a social phenomenon that puts the lives of people, families and families at risk. society.

THE GAMBLER

Thanks for reading

Andrea Falcinelli

TABLE OF CONTENTS

Preface   9

1- Risk adrenaline as a drug   15

2- The neverland in the land of toys   35

3- Doctor Farnesi and his slot machine lover   47

4- Giacomo the "bullied" boy   59

5- Areum Lee the korean entrepreneur   69

6- Iolanda, loneliness and her slot friend   93

7- Harvey "the wolf of walll street"   113

8- A potential subconscious cause:
   childhood and your past   125

9- Society and system the hidden enemies   137

10- The damage of constraints: you have to make
    money! And so you won't make any money   149

11- The orgasm of defeat:
    enjoying when you lose a lot or all   157

12- The chronic gambler profile   165

13- Problems on your psycho-physical health
    Sedentary lifestyle laziness and isolation   173

14- How to get out of gambling or limit it   177

15- Yoga and meditation:
    a miraculous support for freedom   185

16- Some conclusive data and analysis   190

Printed in Great Britain
by Amazon

56997983R00115